D0722270

WILD GIRLS

NORTON
SHORTS

WILD GIRLS

*How the Outdoors Shaped the Women
Who Challenged a Nation*

TIYA MILES

W. W. NORTON & COMPANY
Celebrating a Century of Independent Publishing

page vii: Lucille Clifton, "the earth is a living thing," from *The Book of Light*. Copyright © 1993 by Lucille Clifton. Reprinted with the permission of The Permissions Company, LLC on behalf of Copper Canyon Press, coppercanyonpress.org.

For information about permission to reproduce selections from this book, write to Permissions, W. W. Norton & Company, Inc., 500 Fifth Avenue, New York, NY 10110

For information about special discounts for bulk purchases, please contact W. W. Norton Special Sales at specialsales@wwnorton.com or 800-233-4830

Manufacturing by Lakeside Book Company
Book design by Ellen Cipriano
Production manager: Delaney Adams

The title page and ornaments of this book are set in Trees, a typeface by Katie Holten.

ISBN: 978-1-324-02087-5

W. W. Norton & Company, Inc.
500 Fifth Avenue, New York, N.Y. 10110
www.wwnorton.com

W. W. Norton & Company Ltd.
15 Carlisle Street, London W1D 3BS

1 2 3 4 5 6 7 8 9 0

For all the eco girls out there wading through the cultural wilds—past, present, and future.

And in loving memory of Helen Hill, Karen Zwick, and Andy Holleman, Harvard College class of 1992.

the earth is a living thing

is a black shambling bear
ruffling its wild back and tossing
mountains into the sea

is a black hawk circling
the burying ground circling the bones
picked clean and discarded

is a fish black blind in the belly of water
is a diamond blind in the black belly of coal

is a black and living thing
is a favorite child
of the universe
feel her rolling her hand
in its kinky hair
feel her brushing it clean

—Lucille Clifton,
    "the earth is a living thing,"
    from *The Book of Light*

CONTENTS

PREFACE: ICE BRIDGES

WHEN I WAS a child, my father took me to the river—the mighty Ohio, named for an Iroquoian word translated as "beautiful river" or "great river." The Ohio is the fourth largest river in North America as measured by flow, yet it is the only one among the major rivers that does not release directly into an ocean. The Ohio does not act alone. It seeks out company. To reach the Atlantic, the Ohio needs a partner, someone to join with. The Mississippi River provides that service, receiving the waters of the Ohio, which contribute 40 percent of the Mississippi's volume. As it stretches to touch the fingers of its sister river, the Ohio moves east to west in a "continental temperate" climate zone marked by moistness in the air across the seasons. Winter temperatures range from a mean of 19.4°F to 50°F (-7°C to 10°C). And sometimes, this large and unusually interdependent river solidifies in places. It freezes, becoming its own bridge between disparate flats of land, between regions we have named Ohio and Kentucky, the North and the South. The Ohio froze more commonly in the nineteenth century than in the twentieth, but even now some of us remember the sight of a formidable river transformed into a wintry walkway and the sense of the impossible becoming possible in a frigid landscape of enchantment.

I feel a closeness with that bridge of a river, with that liquid link to other lands and potentialities. As a preschooler growing up in Cincinnati, I contracted an infection caused by fungal spores that are partial to the Ohio River valley; as a result, I lost most of the sight in one eye. In a way, we might say that water channel disabled me, but in truth, it also enabled my life of imagination. When I was a little older, I walked on that water that had created the conditions for my impaired sight. In January of 1977, when I was seven, Cincinnati saw its second coldest winter on record. Twenty-eight days below zero, in which the low reached −25°F, led to a river freeze 12 inches thick. The winters of 1977 and 1978 were two among the fourteen times that the Ohio River froze since scientific recording began in 1874. The Ohio River has not frozen like that in over forty years. Given the reality of climate change, it is unlikely to do so ever again.

My father took me and my little sister down to the river that first frozen year, saying he wanted us to walk on the water. I recall my trepidation and exhilaration at stepping onto the dangerous Ohio, transformed into a crystal sheet beneath my boots. And I recall the gift my father gave me that day: the courage that comes from meeting a natural entity that could swallow you up, but chooses instead to hold you. I did not know then that this was a storied river with a history of bearing enslaved Black people to freedom. The tragic and highly publicized story and legal case of Margaret Garner, a woman seeking liberty in the 1850s, had been famous

in the nineteenth century. It had, however, faded from public consciousness until Toni Morrison used it as inspiration for her stunning novel, *Beloved*.

Margaret Garner had been born an enslaved girl in Kentucky,
near the Ohio River. Like the formerly enslaved writer Harriet
Jacobs, she experienced sexual predation in her teenage years. The
man who owned Margaret, Archibald Gaines, took advantage of her
vulnerability and his power. By the time she was twenty-two, Margaret had four children. She had been permitted to informally marry
a local enslaved man named Robert Garner—informal because the
law did not recognize marriage between unfree people. Margaret's
four children were likely fathered by both men, and her youngest sur-
viving child, according to witnesses, looked nearly white. When she
found herself pregnant with a fifth child, perhaps something inside
Margaret's spirit snapped. She decided, in a state of desperation and
daring, to partner with the Ohio River. On "one of the coldest days
on record for Kentucky," January 28, 1856, Margaret and Robert
Garner fled with all the children and Robert's parents, seeking relief
from captivity. Because the river was frozen over that month, the
family could cross it on foot. The Ohio had become what newspaper
accounts at the time called an "ice bridge" or a "winter bridge." The
Garners were not alone in making a bid for freedom that January
night. Nine other enslaved people along the Ohio also escaped in
what the *Chicago Tribune* disparagingly called a "stampede of slaves."

The story had a tragic end for the Garner family. They crossed
the river and reached the home of Margaret's free relatives in Ohio,
but their reprieve was brutally brief. With armed officers by his side
and the Fugitive Slave Act at his back, Archibald Gaines stormed
the house and recaptured them. Margaret attempted to take the life

of her children before allowing them to be returned to Gaines as his property. She killed the youngest child and was put on trial. The court returned Margaret Garner and her family to Archibald Gaines, who immediately sold them down river into the Deep South. Soon after this heartbreaking episode, Philadelphia-based African American writer, abolitionist, and feminist Frances Ellen Watkins Harper composed a poem titled "The Slave Mother: A Tale of the Ohio" (1857), which describes Margaret Garner traversing a river "bridged and spanned with ice."

Others did make it to lasting freedom by walking the frozen river. In 1893, former US president Rutherford B. Hayes told W. H. Siebert, the Ohio State University Underground Railroad historian, that in the winters of 1850, 1851, 1852, 1853, 1855, and 1856, "the river was frozen over and crossing made everywhere practicable near Ripley and Cincinnati." When Hayes recited these dates, he added political context, noting that this was "soon after the fugitive slave law" had passed. The Fugitive Slave Act of 1850 permitted the recapture of fugitives in the North and mandated citizen cooperation with their forcible return, while severely penalizing those who aided self-liberating Black people. The federal law sent shockwaves of fear through free Black communities, where many former captives resided even as the law both targeted and radicalized abolitionists of all racial backgrounds.

The freezing of the Ohio River for nearly five years straight after the passage of the Fugitive Slave Act encouraged more enslaved people to escape, often in groups, at a critical moment that saw a gathering of social momentum leading up to the Civil War. We could say that the Ohio River froze throughout the 1850s entirely by chance. But there are other possibilities visible only through a lens of ecological enchantment. This wily river was my inheritance as a Black girl outdoors in the 1970s. As a Black woman writer today, it is my inspiration, a reminder that despite the traumas of history and amid the trials of our current times, nature can be a bridge that holds us, joins us, and aids us.

Bozeman, MT, May 2022

WILD GIRLS

WAY FINDERS

———

Where were the Black stories of freedom and
possibility forged on the trail?

—Carolyn Finney, "Who Gets Left Out of the 'Great
Outdoors' Story?" *New York Times*, 2021

Where were the girls?

—Ashley E. Remer and Tiffany R. Isselhardt,
Exploring American Girlhood, 2021

I GREW UP IN many different natures. I'll tell you about just two.
In the early 1970s, my mother and I lived with my grandparents
in their sturdy brick house in a Black working-class neighborhood
of the urban Midwest. My grandmother's dead-end street and the
perpendicular lane that bisected it presented a vast world, it seemed,
of adventure and delight. I tromped back and forth from girlfriend's
yard to girlfriend's yard, playing Candy Land and Monopoly on
front porches, jumping rope and skipping hopscotch on the pave-
ment, and catching lightning bugs in jars until somebody's mother or
grandmother or aunt began the chorus to call us in. Those weekend

and summertime days seemed to stretch into millennia, and the handful of yards in which we played seemed an infinite domain. It was as if we owned that street, a handful of brown girls, but of course we didn't. Physical and psychological threat lurked around every corner. This was the same street where my friend's mother would get drunk, lurch out to rage in her misery, and send us scattering while our playmate bore the brunt of her heat. It was the place where an older boy on his bike knocked down a toddler-aged me, causing an injury that my grandmother mistakenly believed was responsible for my legal blindness in one eye. This was also the street bordered by another that I was told never to cross, a directive that I instinctively obeyed. Our technicolor play world stopped at that corner where our side of Mitchell Avenue abutted the other side, where wealthy white people lived in massive houses with lawns like parks. I did not dare to walk those streets in the northern portion of the neighborhood until I was grown. And even then, I felt the prick of suspicious stares on my back. This nature of my grandmother's street was candy coated and sun streaked, but it existed inside a bubble that, by the time I was a teenager, I knew would pop. The outdoors of that neighborhood, while sponsoring an exuberance that I will always cherish, could only pretend to guarantee safety and could not forever disguise its limits.

If the nature beyond my grandmother's porch was bursting with girlish companionship, the nature past my mother's stoop was cold and lonely. Once my mother was able to afford the rent, the two of us moved to a housing development in an outer ring of the city. This low-income complex was colloquially known as "Single Mothers' Row" and officially named Glen Meadows. I remember how vast the outdoors seemed at the Row—with the L-shaped, two-story, shared-wall units arranged around a parking lot, the hardscape playground tucked to one side, and the green space behind the building that formed a long, shared yard. I had no friends here at first, and I crisscrossed the parking lot, common yard, and playground on my own, finding in those segmented spaces many untold marvels, like a robin's nest with jewel-like eggs, a shrub broad enough to crawl inside, and green glass-bottle shards that glowed in the sunlight. One weekend when it was especially quiet on the Row, I roamed farther out than I ever had, beyond the built environment of the complex, to the wide, grassy field on the edge of the block that stood between our buildings and no-woman's land. Past the meadow there were only trees that urban development had yet to penetrate. This was the field, I had been told, where the high school kids went at night to guzzle beer and get pregnant. I made my way toward it, into it, just to stand alone for a while in the waving grasses that seemed to want me. I remember how the meadow felt—big, so big, all-encompassing, like my idea of an ocean. Still, I waded into it, afraid that I would lose my bearings and not know how to find my way back again. I got so far into the meadow that it was as though I had entered an elsewhere. There were no streets here, no lines not to cross, no houses, and no voices calling me back from the edge. I don't know how long I stayed, or what time of day it was, but I do retain a sense-memory of light softly fading into grass. I froze in place as I spotted a brown rabbit and white flash of tail, then two, then three. The rabbits converged not far from me, formed a kind of circle, and seemed to move in unison. As I watched them for what felt like a long moment, but may have only been seconds, I was sure that they were dancing. And in that instant, I knew wonder was possible, especially at the edges where distinct zones meet.

I trusted one person with the story, someone more familiar with the meadow than I. This was my cousin, a curious, adventurous, brown-skinned girl, named, like me, after our grandmother. She had moved in with us when the necessity arose, and she was, rumor around the complex had it, one of those high school kids who frequented the field for less than scientific purposes. As we sat cross-legged on her champagne-colored sateen comforter, we took up the urgent questions at hand. Did rabbits sometimes secretly dance, and had I been permitted to witness this? My cousin listened intently to my story, weighing the evidence while popping her gum. Maybe she thought the odd tale was a figment of my fanciful mind or a trick of my compromised eyesight. But she didn't say so. Instead, she nodded with the wisdom of a sage seventeen-year-old. Anything was possible in the glen.

I left that nature sighting and the conversation that followed feeling fascinated and empowered by two realizations. Nature was a place apart, but not so far apart that we human beings were unwelcome there. And in these semi-wild spaces on the edges of our built and known environments, life followed different rules. While outdoors, a girl who could not confidently swim might plunge into an imaginary field of ocean; a girl who felt lonely might sense a flash of kinship with other small, earnest mammals; and woodland creatures caricatured as rampant baby-makers, much like the women of Single Mothers' Row, might practice a hidden culture of communion, freedom, and joy. Crossing an invisible border into a domain that I associated with "out there" and glimpsing the rabbit inhabitants forever changed my outlook. I learned that the unexpected, the impossible, and even the magical could occur outside.

I lived at Glen Meadows for a few years in grade school while my mother worked in a department store during the day, studied to attain her associates degree by night, and searched for a job that would provide us with health care benefits. As my mother and I moved into different housing over the years, eventually living in a brick row house (the first that my mother ever owned) in the West End of the city near downtown, I never stopped exploring outdoors. It was a favorite solo activity of mine to walk the tight sidewalks, scanning the colorful streetscapes of buildings, yards, residents, and pets; to poke into abandoned lots and watch butterflies land on weeds; and to sneak through the ruins of condemned houses from a century past. These were the places that sparked my interest in people's historical lives and began the spin of stories in my mind that would shape my career as a scholar and writer.

In the lives of the historical girls and women at the center of this book, outside also presented new possibilities, as enclosure indoors most often meant the restrictive domestic sphere of the idealized home and its concomitant Victorian gender ideology tied to racial hierarchy, Christian virtue, and restrained bodily comportment. This idealized and constraining domestic space also included the Southern plantation house, where a subset of enslaved African American girls ("house servants") labored against their will for others. It included, as well, the federal American Indian boarding school, where generations of Native American girls, removed from their tribal contexts through questionable means, studied how to become "civilized" to a Euro-American Christian standard. By the early 1800s, as Victorian ideology took hold in American society, these diverse populations of girls—"white," "black," and "red"— were all relegated, albeit in different ways and with more and less severe consequences, to stilted "indoors" spaces characterized by a combined physical, architectural, and cultural confinement. In various ways necessitated by their circumstances and social positions, girls who managed to reverse this condition of domestic confinement and get outside—to move, play, journey, explore, escape, and push themselves physically and mentally—were able to expand their minds, test their grit, develop their skills, and profoundly alter the course of their lives. Finding these girls in their outdoor moments is the aim of this little book. The quest requires not only noticing girls outside, but also parsing their various ways of being outdoors in the context of cultural assumptions in their time and ours about femininity and race.

For Euro-American middle-class girls, spending time outside in vigorous exertion was counter to expectations about proper feminine behavior. Yet others, especially Black adolescent girls and women, were associated with a narrow kind of outdoor activity—exploitative fieldwork that required physical strength and overshadowed their femininity. Meanwhile, Native American girls and women were linked to idealized landscapes in American cultural mythology: the Land O'Lakes brand Indian maiden set against a bucolic natural background, though recently retired, is ingrained in the mainstream imagination. Recognizing that girls in these groups thought, felt, and moved outside will require not only identifying how, where, and to what effect, but also expanding and at times correcting commonly held cultural narratives and images.

Western philosophy has tended to associate all women with unfettered nature (as opposed to the masculinized arenas of reason and culture), thereby romanticizing and sexualizing them. Nonetheless, ironically, American cultural practices in the past denied actual women the right to freedom of movement and daring adventure in outdoor space. But Euro-American girls enjoyed getting lost, getting dirty, and testing societal rules; African American girls cherished and interpreted beautiful phenomena in the natural world around them; and Native American girls felt spiritually and somatically connected to their homelands even as they critically assessed the grounded realities of American settlement. None of these groups of girls was passive in their environment, predictably feminine or masculine in their expression of physicality, fully immersed within nature, or fully separated from it.

By thinking and acting outside, these girls who matured into women bent the future of the country toward freedom—for the enslaved, the colonized, the dispossessed, the sequestered, the suppressed, and the subjugated. In retrospective writing, some of these influential women would use the language of "wildness" to express a powerful attachment to free outdoor space, characterized by holistic physical activity and guided by naturalistic philosophy. Wild girls in their youth, they had become fully attuned to the shifting dynamics of nature, power, and place.

My intellectual interest in Black women in nature traces back to 2005, when I realized, through conversation with the sociologist and award-winning environmental studies scholar Dorceta Taylor that Harriet Tubman would have had a pronounced ecological consciousness. To survive enslavement, mastermind escapes across "wild" spaces in Maryland, and treat soldiers with botanical remedies sourced herself as a Civil War nurse in South Carolina, Tubman must have closely observed and understood her natural surrounds.

Indeed, Black feminist ideas on the importance of place as well as nature to identity formation, historical understanding, and political analysis form the bedrock of this book.

Just as critical to this study are stories of Indigenous girlhood, rooted in my previous scholarship and teaching on African American and Native American intertwined histories and on Native women's histories. The outdoor stories of Euro-American girls are drawn from a course I taught on abolitionist women's activism: these white reformers, once children who pondered the midwestern stars and rolled down the northeastern hills, joined the struggle to end slavery and racial prejudice before taking up the fight for women's suffrage. Together, the girls featured here, some famous and others who should be better known, make up a newly conjoined cast of historical actors who navigated their *social* world differently because of their experience in the *outdoor* world.

Girls had rich lives outdoors, but history has largely overlooked them, distracted, perhaps, by famous boy figures like Mark Twain's Huck Finn. Time spent outdoors honed girls' modes of thought and fields of action, propelling them toward creative imaginings and physical activities that seemed impossible at a time when African American girls could be bought and sold like property, Native American girls could be forcibly schooled toward the goal of assimilation, Euro-American girls could be sequestered in domestic space, and all girls were being conditioned for gendered submission to the father, the preacher, the husband, the slave master, the schoolmaster, or the Indian agent. Certainly, the argument that outdoor life shaped girls' characters in profound ways and toward transformative outcomes cannot hold for all girls in United States history, but it partially explains the adult feats of some women willing to test society's norms. Outside spaces in many forms—woods, prairies, mountains, fields, rivers, yards, parks, lots, streets, and more—became, for these renegade girls, imagination stations and training grounds.

"Outdoors" is a vast and variegated category. Decades of environmental history scholarship has questioned the notion of a pure "wilderness," documented the overlap between human space and "natural" space, and pointed out the omnipresence of "nature" in all aspects of human society (from urban centers, to industrial products, to the human body itself). Yet many readers, and even some nature writers and enthusiasts, still see the "outdoors" as a narrow kind of zone that exists only in rural and wild places and is peopled solely by white outdoorsmen and outdoorswomen who emphasize conservation or by white rural families with a dedication to what is often termed "traditional values." African Americans are rarely conceived as residents of rural America or as participants in a National Parks community, even as Black urban outdoor spaces are rarely rendered as natural in popular culture. This erasure stems, in large part, from how Americans see—or do not see—people of color in relation to the natural world of the past. In the national historical imagination, African Americans are recalled as picking cotton on Southern plantations; Mexican Americans are visualized plucking fruit on West Coast farms; Asian Americans are remembered for building railroad track in the West; and Native Americans are overidentified with a romantic notion of wilderness conquered with the closing of the proverbial frontier. Girls, especially girls of color and girls with disabilities and chronic illnesses, are hardly imagined outside at all.

While it is true that political, social, and economic forces have shaped who can be out of doors, at what times, in what capacities, and at what cost to their lives, it is also the case that people imagined to exist outside only as exploited laborers or romanticized symbols have, in fact, lived large and impactful lives outdoors. Theirs is a natural world that is simultaneously "wild" and built. It cuts through cities as well as the countryside, encompasses water and sky as well as land, and is broad, expansive, and fully vital, penetrating even into the interior realms of the imagination.

From the micro scale of a single tree to the macro scale of the forest, spaces in nature have been meaningful to the visionary lives of American girls. Girl-outsiders became trailblazers in their communities and American culture writ large. Time in the outdoors ignited girls' critical awareness, fed their self-knowledge, charged their imaginations, built their capacity for resilience, and bestowed moments of inner peace that steadied their spirits in tumultuous times. The stories pressed into this book like wildflower petals will show how time spent outside shaped the character of girls who later changed the country. Through their wide-ranging ways of going out, girls became sharper in mind and deed, developing skills and honing ideas that they later applied in challenging circumstances. Being outdoors permitted girls, consigned to cloistered domestic and ideological space, a means to experience freedom of physical movement, to escape adult surveillance, and to explore beyond gendered societal dictates—a space to discover who they were and what they were capable of. This relative license (inflected by the complexities of enslavement, race, culture, indigeneity, and class) fueled girls' sense of self-definition and potential.

While this book proposes that the out-of-doors lit girls' imaginations, tested their talents, and readied them for social courage and political action, it also portrays outside as a dual and even dialectical space where brightness joined darkness, wonder met worry, and exploration was tethered to danger. The history of girls outdoors, especially girls of color, reveals a persistent shadow side, where labor exploitation and physical danger haunted daily life. With attention to the many kinds of outdoor spaces that girls moved through, this take emphasizes girls' experiences of nature as relational. All the girls in this book faced constraints and crises of ranging proportions. Amid these trials, they went outside—sometimes by force, other times by choice. They struggled with, communed with, and fell in love with the outdoors and the many living things (trees, plants, animals) and abiotic features (stars, water bodies, ball courts) encountered there.

The girls profiled in these pages lived through times more dangerous and tumultuous (so far) than ours. They were born into legalized slavery and entrenched systems of racial subjugation, into the chaos of an expanding Eurocentric nation that threatened their people's sovereignty and well-being, into a society that suppressed all women and refused them the right to control their own bodies and lives. They matured into adulthood during the abolitionist movement, Indian removal, the Civil War, Reconstruction, Jim Crow, and the allotment era. As women activists, writers, and teachers, as family members and community members, they fought for freedom, equality, and citizenship rights despite the thickets of political exclusion and repression that entangled them. As young people, they welcomed the natural world as an ally; nature, in turn, lent them comfort, inspiration, and insight. In our moment, there is a pressing need for everyone who values freedom to seek common cause with one another and the earth. I offer this work not only as a foray into the past world of American girls and the meanings they made outside, but also as a field guide for any watchful reader who tracks the stars and wonders, with a quixotic mix of audacity and awe, where those faint lights might lead. History tells us that change is possible when people find ways through the fog.

The trail is calling. Are you ready?

CHAPTER 1

STAR GAZERS

———

MINTY ROSS WAS an amphibious girl, born into land and water and destined through strife and experiment to mature into mastery of both domains. Her storied life, replete with drama and singular daring, would be punctuated by her intimate relationship with plants, trees, and waterways. "I grew up like a neglected weed, ignorant of liberty, having no experience of it," she confided to an interviewer long after she had adopted the new name of Harriet Tubman. And even as Tubman, the celebrated Underground Railroad operative, linked herself to a type of plant in this summary statement of her childhood experience, she and her foremothers shared an uncomfortable closeness with water. Tubman's grandmother, an African woman called Modesty, had been transported to the United States on a transatlantic slaving vessel. Modesty's daughter, Harriet "Rit" Green, would be born into slavery in Maryland, a waterlogged coastal state in the Upper South that bordered the landlocked northern state of Pennsylvania. In 1822, a dauntless daughter, Araminta "Minty" Ross—who later became famous, and in some circles, infamous, for leading several escapes from captivity—was born on the Eastern Shore of the Chesapeake Bay to Rit and her husband, Ben Ross.

Harriet Tubman connected the memory of her younger self with a wild and unwanted plant as she told her life story because, she claimed, weeds had no awareness of bondage and freedom. Yet, her choice to compare herself to a weed reveals much more than her owners' attempt to keep her ignorant of the entitlements that white people shared. Weeds may be disparaged by humankind (the single characteristic that binds them together as a class of plant), but they are hardy, persistent, and resilient. They consistently prove themselves capable of extracting nutrients from the soil and processing light from the sun in hostile, human-sculpted environments. Weeds are difficult to contain and to kill. Controlling them is a battle, as Harriet must have known from the farms where she was held captive and the gardens she may have been assigned to weed.

Disdained by resident humans who shared the arbitrary trait of whiteness and excessive power over her and her family members, Harriet Tubman, much like a weed, found the potential for growth and strength in the landscape of exploitation into which she was born, cut into the dense woods and tidal swamps of the Chesapeake Bay. As Karen Hill, director of the Harriet Tubman Home in New York put it in an interview, Tubman "was able to separate the brutality of slavery from how she loved the land."

As a child growing up in the fertile, damp, forested lands of rural Maryland, Harriet Tubman lived as much outdoors as indoors. She chafed at the requirements of domestic production and household service and dreaded being cornered in rooms where enslavers could more readily surveil and mistreat her. Tubman resisted learning how to weave, for instance. According to her biographer, Sarah Bradford, who published chronicles of Tubman's life with Tubman's cooperation to raise funds for the activist: "She would not learn, for she hated her mistress, and did not want to live at home, as she would have done as a weaver, for it was the custom then to weave cloth for the family . . . in the house." For Black girls and young women, laboring indoors beneath the noses of exacting mistresses and under the gazes of lascivious masters made for stifling, threat-filled days. Tubman preferred being outside even as she had little choice to elect where she could go as an unfree child. Later, the outdoors became her primary workplace by assignment of a series of owners who recognized her aptitude for field, farm, and forest labor. In nature Harriet Tubman found a space both raw and changeable, a prison where she was forced to produce and a classroom where she could learn and grow.

Libraries and archives do not contain personal reflections or correspondence written by Tubman herself. Instead, there are dictated letters, snatches of memory, and lyrics to the songs she sang as written and preserved by people who knew her, predominantly white women who supported her causes and recorded her words in their approximation of a Black vernacular dialect. Still, the corpus of written material created during Tubman's lifetime amounts to what the Tubman biographer Jean Humez has called a "self-expressive legacy" stemming from Tubman's insistence on telling, performing, and dictating her own personal stories before private and public audiences. In these filtered memories, Harriet Tubman appears familiar with her physical environment and connected to the natural world. "The outdoors, which she grew to love," writes the historian and Tubman biographer Erica Dunbar, "became her sanctuary."

One of Tubman's earliest memories was of the deciduous gum

trees that fanned across the old fields and pine forests of the Chesapeake Bay. Tubman recalled in her reminiscences to Emma Telford, a white neighbor who narrated Tubman's life story based on first-hand conversations around the year 1905:

> In eastern shore of Maryland Dorchester County is where I was born. The first thing I remember, was lying in de cradle. You seen these trees that are hollow. Take a big tree, cut it down, put a bode in each and, make a cradle of it and 'call it a 'gum [*sic*]. I remember lying in that there.

Perhaps Tubman's enslaved father, Ben Ross, who worked in the timber trade at his owner's behest, had carved this wooden cradle, transforming a feature of the forest into a means and symbol of parental care. Yet, as one of Tubman's biographers, Kate Clifford Larson, has pointed out, the spherical seedpods of the sweet gum tree so common to Tubman's surroundings turned sharp and dangerously prickly after they had fallen to the ground. The droppings of these trees could puncture bare feet—Tubman's own and those of people she would later aid in their escapes from bondage. As a child who walked the forest floor while going about her required tasks and sneaking out late at night to visit her mother, Harriet Tubman learned that nature wore at least two faces. It could soothe the soul and give shelter, like the smooth wooden cradle in which she rocked as in infant, and it could cause suffering, like the seedpods of that same tree species. The sweet gum cradle elicited a memory of pleasure tinged with melancholy for Tubman, even as the sweet gum trees that likely served as landmarks on her treacherous routes north laced that same path with thorns.

Throughout her youth, Harriet Tubman would experience nature as a multifaceted and mysterious surround. The world outside was teacher and tormentor, protector and saboteur. She observed her mother defiantly use the woods as a hiding place to shield a son from sale, and she watched her father expertly manage the forest as a skilled harvester of its bounty. As a child and later, a young adult, she would follow her parents' examples and begin to intentionally use nature—first animals, then trees, plants, and waterways, as tools of resistance to enslavement and abuse. Tutored by parents who espoused a Black Christian faith, and exposed to the many religious traditions in her multiracial, multiethnic community (including Methodism, Catholicism, Quakerism, and African spiritual belief), Tubman expanded her material orientation to the natural world to cosmic dimensions and began to experience outdoor spaces, particularly the woods, as sacred realms for communion with the God in whom she fervently trusted. Each of these ways of relating to nature—as hideout, tool, resource, and sacred space—prepared Tubman to become the woman others would come to call "Moses," navigating the outdoors in wonder and power with the aid of her liberating God.

When Harriet was born, the middle child of nine, her grieving parents had already lost children to the slave market at the hands of Rit's owners, the Brodess family. Rit and Ben Ross had wed after the two were brought together by the marriage of their enslavers, Mary Pattison Brodess and her second husband, Dr. Anthony Thompson. As fertile soils were exhausted and the tobacco economy faltered, slaveholders began looking to other financial opportunities. At the same time, cotton agriculture and production extended farther south and west into the rich lands of Native American nations that would be seized by the United States in the Indian removal era of the 1820s and 1830s. White opportunists migrating into these newly opened lands sought to enlarge their labor forces. For slaveholders in the Upper South, unfree Black people represented easy "capital," and in addition to profiting from their labor, slaveowners sought to realize the wealth stored in the bodies of their legal slaves. Some sold individuals southward, separating families. Many hired African Americans out to others who could use their labor on a temporary basis. Slaveholders also diversified their economic operations, developing a flourishing timber industry that forcibly employed unfree people like Harriet Tubman's father, Ben, and later, Harriet herself. Edward Brodess, the son of Mary Brodess and the owner of Harriet Tubman's mother and hence of Harriet and her siblings, employed all three of these income-building strategies. As the shape of chattel bondage shifted in Maryland, so did the makeup of the state's population and the daily labor practices of rural life. The percentage of free African Americans in Maryland increased, through manumission (being liberated legally by the people who owned them) as well as through escape. As enslaved Blacks were increasingly being leased out to live and work beyond the estates of their legal owners, more of them were able to escape to live in the large port city of Baltimore.

Harriet Tubman grew up bearing the brunt, and seeing the possibilities, in these changing economic and social dynamics. Her owner repeatedly leased Harriet and her siblings to others on distant estates. When she was only six or seven, Harriet was sent 10 miles from home to labor for James Cook and his wife, a harsh and demanding couple. There she was made to perform all manner of work inside and out, including wading through the cold, brackish waters to collect muskrats from the traps Cook had placed so that he could sell the creatures' pelts into a lucrative fur market. She fell ill with the measles at the Cook farm and was sent home, where her mother nursed her back to health only to have their owner lease Harriet out once more, this time sending her to the household of a white woman, Miss Susan, who wanted someone at "low wages" to tend her infant ("wages" that would go to her owner's family). Because Harriet, not yet ten, could not keep the baby quiet or the furniture dusted to Susan's satisfaction, she was beaten regularly and unmercifully and bore the scars for the rest of her life. Once she snuck a cube of sugar and then, when she saw Susan reach for the whip, fled and hid in a pigpen on a nearby farm for four to five days. Harriet slept and ate with "eight or ten little pigs" and their mother until she became afraid that the "old sow" would harm her for taking too much food from the trough. Hungry, dirty, and exhausted, Harriet returned to Susan's household and was "shamefully beaten," she would later recall, by the man of the house. Harriet paid a terrible price for her recalcitrance, but she also learned at a young age that if she were daring enough and willing to risk deprivation and punishment, she could survive for days on her own outdoors.

Harriet Tubman was not alone in grasping at nature to withstand the unexpected blows of slavery. Other African American girls also saw the outdoors as a source of physical and psychological relief. Kate Drumgoold, who had grown up near the city of Petersburg, Virginia, at the time of the Civil War, published the brief memoir *A Slave Girl's Story* in 1898. She lived with her mother and several siblings on the estate of the elderly woman who owned them. Drumgoold contended that while her sisters were hired out and learned through the rental of their bodies what it meant to be slaves, she was never treated as a "servant." Yet, the two central memories that stood out from her childhood—a fire that destroyed her family's cabin and the sale of her mother—reveal the vulnerability of her status and the trauma of her personal history. "My dear mother was sold at the beginning of the war from all of her little ones," Kate Drumgoold wrote, "after the death of the lady that she belonged to, and who was so kind to my dear mother and all of the rest of the negroes on this place." While protecting the reputation of this unnamed woman, Kate criticized the motives for the sale. "The money that my mother was sold for was to keep the rich man from going to the field of battle, as he sent a poor white man in his stead." Her mother, carried off while the children were unaware, was taken to doubly preserve the wealth and lifestyle of slaveholders.

While a buyer carted her mother off to Georgia, Kate was overwhelmed by confusion. "We did not know that she was sold until she was gone," she remembered, "and the saddest thought was to me to know which way she had gone." In the wake of her mother's sudden seizure, Kate began to fixate on a single feature in her world that was beyond the reach of the slave market. "I used to go outside and look up to see if there was anything that would direct me, and I saw a clear place in the sky, and it seemed to me the way she had gone, and I watched it three and a half years, not knowing what that meant, and it was there the whole time my mother was gone from her little ones." Kate reported that this bright spot remained in place for nearly four years, a claim that could not have been objectively possible. But inside Kate's mind, that clear patch did remain steady. She had turned to the sky in her search for moorings and imagined that a patch of blue represented her lost parent. The brightness in the sky, like a portal to hopes, was her psychic reassurance that she was not alone.

Kate Drumgoold was among the fortunate minority of enslaved children who reunited with their parents following the Civil War. She and some of her siblings still resided in the area where they had been enslaved, which enabled her mother to locate them. On the day of their reunion, nature seemed to miraculously produce her parent. "On one bright Sunday I asked my older sister to go with me for a nice walk," Kate recalled. "And we saw some sweet flowers on the wayside and we b[e]gan to have delight in picking them, when all at once I was led to leave her alone with the flowers and to go where I could look up at that nice, clear spot, and as I wanted to get as near to it as I could, I got on the fence, and as I looked that way I saw a form coming to me that looked like my dear mother's." Kate Drumgoold's mother had returned with the seeming magic of a sky goddess. She had come to save the children, and she had secured the help of a Union officer to move them to the North. For Kate, the sky had stood in for this lost parent and ultimately produced her again. Linking her imagination up with the natural world had been a balm to Kate's spirit during the pain of separation.

Like Kate Drumgoold, the young Harriet Tubman would lose loved ones and contemplate the state of the sky. For both girls, the sky above could be a source of comfort and terror even as it offered ultimate proof that human masters did not control the earth and everything upon it. In the 1830s, Harriet Tubman observed a series of terrifying and miraculous events that made strong impressions on her young mind about human limitations and cosmic scale. This was the likely decade when Brodess sold two of Harriet's sisters and attempted to sell her youngest brother, Moses. Harriet's mother, Rit, defied her master, running with Moses to the woods and hiding him there for a month, eventually thwarting the sale. But the sold-away

daughters could not be recovered, and the loss of them haunted Tubman, who had recurring nightmares about family members taken
and the anguish of those left behind.

Harriet was around eleven years old on "the night the stars
fell." Having learned the hard way that she could steal away tem-
porarily without being found, Harriet would sneak out at night to
see her mother, who had been hired out to work on another farm.
While Harriet visited with Rit inside the cabin, one of her brothers
would stand guard outside to watch for white men who patrolled
the roads, hunting for slaves out of place. On this night, her brother
suddenly summoned Harriet, urging her to "come out and see the
stars!" Harriet exited the cabin, peered into the darkness, and saw
the stars "all shooting whichway." In that moment she thought "the
end of the world had come." She was witness to the spectacular and
widely reported astrological event known as the 1833 Leonid meteor
storm. Overnight on November 12 and 13, approximately one hundred thousand fiery, white "stars" plummeted toward the earth like
a cascade of firecrackers. Across the country, those who witnessed
the shower of stars (in actuality, particles cast off from the comet
Tempel-Tuttle) rushed toward religious interpretations of judgment
day or, with an equal zeal, toward rational formulations of the new
field of meteor science. Enslaved people like Harriet and her brother
were among those moved to interpret the event as divine commentary on human affairs.

Jane Clark was one of those fellow stargazers. Years after the
1833 meteor storm, Jane escaped to New York as a young woman
with the assistance of her brother and the Underground Railroad
network. Jane would tell her story to a white neighbor, Julia Ferris,
who wrote it down and read it aloud at a banquet in 1897. Jane Clark

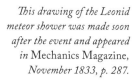

This drawing of the Leonid meteor shower was made soon after the event and appeared in Mechanics Magazine, *November 1833, p. 287.*

was raised in an unnamed Southern state in the home of her maternal grandmother until age six or seven, when she was "taken in payment of a debt." The person who then owned Jane hired her out when she was eight. At this new location, Jane labored "with two other children, to bring water a long distance from a spring for culinary purposes for all on the plantation." Toting containers of heavy water would have been onerous for adults and excruciating for children. As Jane recalled, the youngsters would "start out about four o'clock in the morning make two trips before breakfast four before dinner and one before supper. The hair was worn off their heads by the water pails which the children carried on them." But even while enduring toil such as this, enslaved children could marvel at natural wonders. Jane recounted in her own words that she and her companions saw the "stars fall" at dawn as they carried out this drudgery, a dreamlike moment described by Jane's amanuensis as "vivid in her memory." The most dramatic hours of the Leonid spectacle occurred between 2 a.m. and dawn, the time of day when little Jane and her fellows rose from their mats or dirt floors to collect their owners' drinking and cooking water. "The children were on their way to the spring,"

Julia Ferris recounted in her oral reading of Jane Clark's story. "They were not old enough to be alarmed by the unusual sight but ran along trying to catch the stars as they fell."

As they watched and reached for flaming balls of light overhead, did these unfree children recall the face of a parent lost to slavery? Did they sense a divine spark in the presence of mystery despite the ordeal that was daily life? The wonderment they surely felt was captured in the words of other formerly enslaved children who witnessed this astrological event and described it later in adulthood. One woman, Maria, spoke of how the stars "fell like a sheet and spread over the ground." A man in South Carolina named Wesley Jones recalled: "Heep o' stars fell when I was young." Many enslaved people set their ages from the time "the stars fell," recalling where they were and if they were a "a little girl on the floor" or "a little shirt tail boy." Many also used this spectacular event to mark and recall the sale of relatives. One woman, Lillie Baccus, born in Mississippi and raised by her grandmother after her mother was sold away, shared her grandmother's memory of that surreal night: "Grandma raised us. She was sold twice. She said she run out of the house to pick up a star when the stars fell. They showered down and disappeared."

Some onlookers marveled at the beauty and strangeness of the stars; others saw ominous signs. The incident terrified many eyewitnesses, the young as well as the old. "Everybody thought that the world was coming to an end," reflected Charlotte Foster of South Carolina. "Everybody was scared to death," said Arkansan Betty Hodge. These were refrains running through the testimony of enslaved people who described the meteor shower in oral accounts captured in interviews in the 1930s. "Grandma said she

remembered the stars falling," Lizzie Johnson of Arkansas rec-
ollected. "She said it turned dark and seem like two hours spar-
kles fell. They said stars fell. She said it was bad times. People was
scared half to death."

Stories of how the stars fell and the meanings enslaved people made of this dramatic occurrence circulate among descendants
even today. Angela Walton-Raji, a professional genealogist who has
published guides on how to conduct African American and Native
American family research, reconstructs the history of her own ancestors through oral and documentary accounts. In an essay titled "The
Night the Stars Fell: My Search for Amanda Young," Walton-Raji
retells a story passed down from her great grandmother Amanda,
which came to her by way of an elderly cousin. Enslaved in Tennes-
see as a girl, Amanda had witnessed the meteor shower. Her descendants remembered and retold the tale in Amanda's voice:

> Somebody in the quarters started yellin' in the middle of the
> night to come out to look up at the sky. We went outside and
> there they was a fallin' everywhere! Big stars coming down real
> close to the groun' and just before they hit the ground they would
> burn up! We was all scared. Some o' the folks was screamin',
> and some was prayin'. We all made so much noise, the white
> folks came out to see what was happenin'. They looked up and
> then they got scared, too. But then the white folks started cal-
> lin' all the slaves together, and for no reason, they started tellin'
> some of the slaves who their mothers and fathers was, and who
> they'd been sold to and where. The old folks was so glad to hear
> where their people went. They made sure we all knew what hap-
> pened . . . you see, they thought it was Judgement Day.

The same astrological happening that brought momentary bliss to Jane and her fellow water carriers shook loose invaluable information for Amanda Young's community. Amanda and her fellow enslaved recognized, as their owners also trembled in fear beneath an unleashing sky, that there existed a power greater than white people's mastery. And while shooting stars did not herald freedom on that strange, bright night, a planetary event had revealed their owners' vulnerability and provided them with intelligence about beloved missing kin.

The confounding power of nature could, Amanda Young's story suggests, hog-tie a slaveholder's intimidating influence. Other enslaved people agreed, as indicated by their accounts. Elizabeth Brannon in Arkansas shared the experience of her grandmother who had been "sold more than once" and separated from her own mother "when she was small." This grandmother, dearly recalled in the cadences of the story, "told us about a time when the stars fell. . . . Her master got scared in Virginia. His niece killed herself 'cause she thought the world was coming to an end." Richard Caruthers from Texas commented sharply: "I 'member when the stars fell. We runs and prays, 'cause we thinks its jedgment day. It sure dumb old Debbie Hill, them stars was over his power." Caruthers recognized that his owner confronted the limits of mastery that upside-down night. In a collective African American imagination inspired by the meteor storm, the sense of an awesome ulterior power fused with conceptualizations of God.

Over sixty years after this astonishing event, the gifted quilter Harriet Powers retold the story of the falling stars in her now famous *Pictorial Quilt* housed at the Museum of Fine Arts in Boston. In a square toward the center of the quilt, a series of orange streamers capped by white spheres plunge toward the ground, where appliqued people and animals stare up in amazement. Born into slavery in 1837, Powers was not alive during the meteor shower of 1833. She must have received the story through oral transmission from someone like Tubman, who had witnessed it. Nevertheless, Powers's verbal description of the quilt square captured the cosmic thrust of enslaved people's experience of the event: "The falling of the stars on November 13, 1833. The people were frighten and thought that the end of time had come God's hand staid the stars. The varmints rushed out of their beds." Trouble would come in this world, but God could hold back the heat of the stars.

What did Harriet Tubman think of the starfall that autumn night? Like other enslaved youngsters, she may have been filled with awe or fear. A child wiser and more courageous than her age, she may have wondered, as well, if the day of divine judgment had come. Like Harriet Powers, Harriet Tubman may have seen both danger and reassurance in the event. She may have read it as a sign that God was active in the world. And if so, perhaps she took this to mean that God was prepared to punish enslavers. At the least, the meteor spray was an indication that miracles could take place outdoors.

Harriet Tubman spent her teenage years being hired to employers who gave her grueling agricultural tasks more commonly carried out by men. According to Sarah Bradford, Tubman's first biographer, "Out of door drudgery . . . was put upon her. The labor of the horse and the ox, the lifting of barrels of flour and other heavy weights." And although the work was arduous and the weather surely unrelenting, carrying out these assignments increased Tubman's physical strength and endurance. During this time, Harriet "learned to love the land, where flora and wildlife reflected seasonal change," one of her present-day biographers writes.

When Harriet was around thirteen and hired out to a white man whom she described as the worst in the neighborhood, she shared a fateful moment with a Black boy or teen enslaved on the same property. Harriet had stepped into a small dry goods store with the household's cook to pick up supplies. Meanwhile, the boy abandoned his work on the farm and ran toward the road, followed by the overseer, who pursued him into the local store. There the overseer hurled a 2-pound metal weight but missed his target. The weight collided into Harriet instead, knocking her nearly unconscious. The blow to her skull would lead to what was most likely a form of temporal lobe epilepsy, a lifelong condition. Harriet was sent back to her owner, who tried to sell her but failed due to her poor physical health and seemingly reduced mental capacity. Harriet's mother once again nursed her back to health. But Harriet's brain would not be the same. She was plagued by headaches and random episodes of falling into a sudden sleep from which she could not be awakened. She also experienced intense visions and dreams that she interpreted as having spiritual import and prophetic meaning. Her disability caused by a violent act proved a strength, as it accompanied a religious awakening and may have enhanced the sensation that God was directly communicating with her.

When she was approximately twenty-two, around 1844, Harriet married a free Black man named John Tubman. Sometime in this period of her twenties, she dropped her birth name of Araminta Ross, taking on her mother's first name and her new husband's surname. Harriet also negotiated with her owner gaining his permission to hire herself out and retain some of her earnings. Astute and financially savvy, she used some of her pay to purchase her own pair of oxen, whose muscle power she employed to increase her potential to earn. Tubman began to work for a man whose business was timber and who also employed her father. (Ben Ross had attained his freedom in 1840.) Alongside her father, the foreman of the logging crew, her brothers, and a group of enslaved and free Black men, Harriet became a woodswoman. She learned the features of the forest, likely picking up from her father what leaves, berries, and nuts were edible and in which direction the water flowed. And she noticed, according to a biographer, Catherine Clinton, "that all the streams she knew ran north to south." Learning the woods may have been transformative for Tubman, putting her into a frame of mind that allowed her to access what James Merrell, a historian of the environment, has called "some of the woods' ancient power," referring to the power of the woods in Western culture to confuse and terrify. Merrell writes of early European settlers in the eastern woodlands: "These people were heirs of a tradition that considered the woods a forbidding place. For centuries, Europeans had drawn maps in their minds that set field against forest, order against disorder, light against darkness." Common expressions in the English language retain this sense of foreboding: "We talk of being *bewildered*; we call a neophyte *a babe in the woods*, we worry that someone is *not yet out of the woods*." For Harriet Tubman, in contrast, the forest became a sheltering place that she knew how to breathe in, dream in, and navigate. Before long, Harriet Tubman, who was no babe in the woods, could use the forest against the slave hunter, turning its dark mystery against him.

When Harriet Tubman heard that she and her brothers might be sold to settle debts following the death of Edward Brodess, she put her knowledge of the natural world, as well as her social networks, to immediate use. In September of 1849, she planned an escape that

HARRIET TUBMAN.

This drawing of Harriet Tubman wearing a satchel and holding a rifle pictures her standing outside at a Civil War encampment, circa 1863–1868. Frontispiece of Sarah H. Bradford's Scenes from the Life of Harriet Tubman, *1869.* Courtesy of New York Public Library.

she undertook with two of her brothers, Henry (Harry) and Ben. On this first attempt, her brothers were overcome with anxiety. The young men wished to return, so the siblings aborted their plan. But Harriet ran again soon after and kept on going. She traveled by night and slept in the day, following Polaris, the North Star, to Philadelphia. She was assisted in her escape by white women and men from neighboring Maryland communities. When Tubman crossed "that magic line," dividing the South from the North, she expressed her joy in naturalistic language: "I was free. There was such a glory over everything, the sun came like gold through the trees and over the fields, and I felt like I was in heaven." Tubman would return for her brothers in 1854, hiding with them in a corn crib near their father's home and with his knowledge until the way seemed clear. Over the next decade, she would bring most of her family members and many others out of slavery.

Harriet Tubman traveled to the South approximately thirteen times to free other people after she had attained her own freedom. Historians estimate that she helped from seventy to eighty individuals liberate themselves. Her own reports of her journeys indicate that neither she nor her fellow travelers, including infants and children, were ever recaptured during these journeys. Tubman's remarkable success depended on numerous factors, not least of which were her own striking intelligence and daring, as well as the existence of a multiracial secret network of Underground Railroad activists. Harriet Tubman's knowledge of and relationship with the world outdoors was a significant element of her accomplishment, yet it has too often been overlooked. In an essay about Tubman's "cosmological knowledge," the astronomer Chanda Prescod-Weinstein has noted: "Only with extensive technical skills, including intimate familiarity with the land, and an incredible level of persistence could Tubman have had this kind of success rate." As a child, teenager, and young woman in her twenties, Tubman had learned how to listen to, forage in, and navigate the woods. She later applied her skills to the incredible escapes she carried out through the trees and across the waterways of Maryland's Eastern Shore. She was, in the words of ranger Angela Crenshaw, of the Harriet Tubman Underground Railroad State Park, "the ultimate outdoors woman."

By relying on her intimate knowledge of the seasons, forests, and animal behavior, Tubman made it to Philadelphia, New York, and Ontario while keeping her companions safe. She preferred to travel in wintertime when longer nights afforded the fugitives greater cover through darkness. She followed the North Star to keep her bearings. She sustained herself and companions with wild foods when necessary, hid in swamps, and took shelter beneath large trees in inclement weather. In one of her most dangerous escapes, in which she had an intuition that slave hunters were on the trail of her fleeing party, Tubman suddenly changed course, leading the way into a stream so deep that she called it a river. She mimicked the barred owl's call to signal her companions when it was safe to emerge from hiding and move through the woods, and she may have watched the directional flow of rivers and creeks for navigational information. Above all in her remembrances, Tubman stressed her reliance on the sky, sharing that she "fix[ed] her eyes on the guiding star, and committ[ed] her way unto the Lord." Even as she watched the steady North Star, Tubman's first biographer poetically related, along the way Tubman had "watchers" of her own, "the stars of the night."

While the young Harriet Tubman was stargazing in the 1830s, wondering if the slaveholder's world was coming to an end, a twenty-year-old enslaved woman, Harriet Ann Jacobs, was fleeing to save her life and the lives of her two children. Harriet Jacobs had been born into slavery in Edenton, North Carolina, around the year 1813. Jacobs was only six when her mother died and she learned "by the talk around me, that I was a slave." Her experience after this doubly tragic event—the loss of a mother and the realization of her unfreedom—is dominated by sexual threat, fear of violence, excru-ciatingly mixed emotions of having borne a son and daughter who were also enslaved, the painful observation of the abuse and suffer-ing of others, the endurance of labor exploitation, and the prolonged plight to free herself and her children. Jacobs spent her adolescence struggling against her controlling "master," who sought to sexually subjugate her at fourteen years old.

Jacobs had personal experience of the risk enslaved Black girls encountered at the hands of their owners or other white men who had physical access to their bodies. She refused to willingly submit to the desires of her master and sought to resist by outwitting him, as she recounted in her memoir, *Incidents in the Life of a Slave Girl*, released in 1861 on the eve of the Civil War. The memoir, the most detailed personal account published by an enslaved woman of the South, was scandalous in its time for yanking back the curtain on Southern sexual predation and disclosing the extreme and partic-ular vulnerability of Black girlhood. Jacobs wrote for the explicitly political purpose of rallying white Christian women of the North to the cause of freedom for Black women. Full of references to outdoor experiences, her narrative also shows how Black girls and women felt strongly connected with nature, for better and for worse.

Throughout, Harriet Jacobs writes about her community's environmental context and conveys the emotions of unfree people through nature metaphors and tropes. She describes natural ele-ments that affect enslaved people's daily lives: water, wind, sunshine, starlight, woods, dirt, vines, fruit, and the atmospheric conditions of sky and weather, and she interprets both the blessings and threats of the Southern outdoors. Rivers and swamps are escape routes, hid-ing places, and geographical symbols of political distance between the slave South and free North. Woods and trees offer shade, rest, and sites for sacred ritual, even as they act as shields against the surveillance and scrutiny of enslavers. Leafy and flowering vines represent plenty and prosperity. Berry picking offers momentary pleasure and signifies feminine innocence. The wind is a harbinger of news, change, and potential danger. Stars in the night sky become animated as watchful judges and potential allies in escape.

Jacobs writes most frequently of trees and woods as places of relief, restoration, secrecy, and refuge. She recalls sitting beneath the shade of a tree while sewing and collapsing "on the stump of an old tree" when she is weighed down by depression after realizing that she is pregnant with her first child conceived with an older, wealthy white man. Years later, when she attempts an escape and hears pursuers nearby, Jacobs hides "behind a large tree." Jacobs describes the experiences of other enslaved people who take to the woods and cool down beneath the shelter of tree canopy. She tells of Black women "hid[ing] themselves in woods and swamps" to evade slave patrols and of the faithful attending "their little church in the woods, with their burying ground around it" in the "terrifying" time of white retribution following Nat Turner's 1831 rebellion. Waterways, in addition to forests, could serve as hideouts. Jacobs herself took cover in the Snaky Swamp, dank and crawling with reptiles, during her final escape. "There," the helpful captain of the secret rescue ship commented, "is a slave territory that defies all the laws."

Indeed, a defiance of man-made slave law instilled the natural world with supernatural value to those crushed beneath the weight of racist legislation. Nature abided by the laws of physics, or rather, by the laws of God, a devout Christian like Harriet Jacobs might have believed, and therefore operated above and beyond slavery's human-made systems. Nature could be destructive, too, as Jacobs's text also shows, when enslavers use trees as whipping posts and cotton fields as threats. However, the ultimate autonomy of the natural world meant that storms and floods, drought and disease, could hurt the mighty as well as the weak.

Woods and trees predominate as natural elements in Jacobs's narrative, followed closely by references to sunshine in a bright sky. The sun represents hope, optimism, and ultimately freedom for Harriet Jacobs. Conversely, obfuscated sunlight signifies violence, abuse, and recapture. A frequently quoted passage of Jacobs's memoir features sunlight. To compare the fates of white and Black girls who have been companions since childhood, she turns to the metaphor of a luminous sky. Jacobs observes about a young beauty who is white: "From childhood to womanhood her pathway was blooming with flowers, and overarched by a sunny sky. Scarcely one day of her life had been clouded when the sun rose on her bridal morning." But the lovely Black girl faces a different fate, Jacobs reveals: "How had those days dealt with her slave sister, the little playmate of her childhood? She, also, was very beautiful; but the flowers and sunshine of love were not for her. She drank the cup of sin, and shame, and misery, whereof her persecuted race are compelled to drink." Harriet Jacobs had personally experienced sexual persecution and shame. When she finally escaped her captivity and reached free land in Philadelphia with a fellow runaway, she again turned to sunlight, but this time as a symbol of freedom and hope. "I called Fanny to see the sunrise, for the first time in our lives, on free soil," Jacobs recollects of the moment. "We watched the reddening sky, and saw the great orb come up slowly out of the water, as it seemed. Soon the waves began to sparkle, and every thing caught the beautiful glow. Before us lay the city of strangers. We looked at each other, and the eyes of both were moistened with tears." In this poetic description that carries a sense of spiritual reverie, Jacobs captures her feeling of joy in an ode to the risen sun. This is a language that her white Northern female readership, steeped in sublime passages by writers like Louisa May Alcott and her mentors in the transcendentalist literary movement, would have readily grasped.

Memories of sunlight filter through Harriet Jacobs's mind as she relates this instance of deliverance, but the life outside she describes is replete with painful contrasts. Her narrative also reveals the back hand of nature, which could smart when it made contact. The sunny sky could cloud over, and the river to freedom could take a life. While hiding in her grandmother's shed prior to her permanent escape, Jacobs witnessed a suicide by drowning: "I saw a woman rush wildly by, pursued by two men. She was a slave, the wet nurse of the mistress's children. For some trifling offence her mistress ordered her to be stripped and whipped. To escape the degradation and the torture, she rushed to the river, jumped in, and ended her wrongs in death." For Harriet Jacobs, nature was an omnipresent, multidimensional feature of life. The woods were places of refuge and spiritual rejuvenation; the sun was a source of hope and a symbol of freedom; and the water bodies like rivers and swamps could be routes of escape, sources of harm, or both.

Laura Smith Haviland also knew that nature could offer solutions, cause problems, and, importantly, pose questions. Even for her reform-minded family of northeastern Quakers, Laura Smith, born free and white in 1808, was an unusual girl. She pronounced herself a "skeptic" at the age of five when she began to question the accuracy of the Bible. At six, Laura had turned her attention to the mysteries of the night sky. While watching the stars, she noticed that her family's house "was just in the middle of the world." This struck her as curious, and she began what she described as an investigation. Whenever she traveled with her family overnight, she observed the stars and measured their distance from the point where she stood, and each time, she found herself "at the center of this great world."

Since she knew that every spot could not, in fact, be central, Laura determined that this feeling of centrality was psychological. People wanted to believe themselves at the center of the universe, she concluded, arguing that "the study of astronomy gives ability to look upon the vast universe of thousands of worlds much larger than our own" and furthers the understanding of standpoint. While she may not yet have possessed this sophisticated language as a school-aged child, Haviland reports in her autobiography, *A Woman's Life-Work, Labors and Experiences* (1881), that she recognized a difference in positionality between individual human beings, which would shape their views of the world. During her time outdoors, she had taught herself a lesson in relative orientation that would contribute to her awareness of cultural diversity and social hierarchy.

When she was seven, the family moved to western New York, a "wilderness" in Laura's eyes. In that metaphorical wilderness, she began to recognize how relative positioning played out on the ground. A precocious reader, Laura explored her father's library and became fixated on a criticism of the African slave trade, written by the Quaker writer and preacher John Woolman. She observed an elderly Black man, "Uncle Jeff," being verbally and physically attacked by white children in town as he tried to earn an income by peddling goods on the street. She witnessed another Black man, Ben, being abused by boys, who purposefully set his pants on fire while he slept in the kitchen of the inn where he worked. This assault left severe burns on Ben's body that limited his range of motion thereafter.

Appalled by the "diabolical" and "wicked" acts she had read about in the comfort of her family home and had seen with her own eyes as she walked about her neighborhood, Laura was primed for a religious awakening. At the age of thirteen, she attended a Methodist prayer meeting, although her parents frowned on it. Overcome by emotion after the service, she slipped into her family's corn crib for privacy and noticed the scene around her, where there was "naught but trees and shrubs of the garden below, and the ethereal blue, bedecked with the beautiful moon and sparkling stars." She prayed in solitude that night in a rough shelter for grain storage. This powerful moment of religious conversion would propel Laura Smith Haviland down a long path on which, a decade afterward as a married and hardworking young woman in rural Michigan, she would formally leave the Quaker faith for a radical antislavery Methodist denomination.

Haviland eventually became an intrepid Underground Railroad activist in Michigan, Ohio, Kentucky, and Ontario. She accompanied fugitives on their treks from the Great Lakes into Canada, organized schools for survivors of slavery, hid runaways from their enslavers, and welcomed Black families onto her farm in independent living arrangements.

Laura Smith Haviland is the only white woman whose record of ambition, action, and bravery in the abolitionist movement bears striking similarities with Harriet Tubman's. In the 1840s, 1850s and 1860s, Haviland dedicated her life to assisting enslaved people in their bids for freedom and education, leaving her children in the care of others to live for months and years away from home. She was fiercely religious, trusted in a Christian God, and had dreams that she interpreted as prophetic in her fight against slavery. She traveled to the South once to try to personally accompany an enslaved woman in Kentucky across the Ohio River to freedom. And although that effort failed, it set Haviland apart as the only white woman in the historical record of the Underground Railroad who organized and carried out her own rescue attempt. Like Harriet Tubman, Laura Smith Haviland had a bounty placed on her head by enslavers seeking the return of their human property. Both women revered the radical abolitionist activist John Brown. Like Tubman, Haviland engaged in relief work for African American refugees during and after the Civil War. And while Harriet Tubman earned the reverent name Moses from many in the transnational Black communities of the northeastern United States and Canada, Laura Smith Haviland wrote in her diary that she was once called one of God's "Moses[es]" by an African American man in Michigan.

All three women—Harriet Tubman, Harriet Jacobs, and Laura Haviland—had yet another noteworthy thing in common. In the early 1800s, when slavery and racial animosity were entrenched, they had developed an understanding of social worlds in relation to natural surroundings. In the Southern landscape of chattel slavery, Tubman labored in the fields, woods, and marshes, learning how to find strength, shelter, and wonder in nature, while Jacobs worked in her master's house farther down the coastline, fighting to preserve her freedom of will and to protect her body while dreaming of a girlhood graced by flowers and sunshine. As a free, materially comfortable white child in the North, Laura Smith Haviland knew nothing like the extremity and brutality of Tubman's and Jacobs's childhoods, but she inferred from her observations of the stars that all lives and positions were not equal. In their vastly different social and geographical locations, nature's classroom taught these girls how to question societal beliefs and practices—and sometimes how to evade those who sought to steal life. As women, they all became visible leaders in antislavery circles, but during their trying early years when they faced their first tests, "the midnight sky and the silent stars" were their witnesses.

CHAPTER 2

NATURE WRITERS

———

IF HARRIET TUBMAN grew like a "neglected weed" in the Upper South, Louisa May Alcott came of age in a culture that deemed her a delicate flower. In the early nineteenth century, genteel Victorian America increasingly upheld a social order with distinct masculine and feminine gender roles. The expectation of behavioral differences between boys and girls was especially apparent in the urban towns of traditional New England, where Alcott was raised as a descendant of old, elite families. Born in 1832 to Abigail "Abba" May, a member of a distinguished Boston clan, and to Bronson Alcott, a starry-eyed, erratically paid philosopher, educator, and public speaker, Louisa May Alcott had a childhood full of twists and turns perhaps equal to those in the novels she would later write. But despite strained family finances and peripatetic residential patterns, Louisa and her three sisters were raised in a white Christian household that espoused a culturally middle-class set of mores.

In the words of a lifelong friend, Maria Porter, Alcott's "childhood and early girlhood were passed in the pure sweet atmosphere of a home where love reigned." As a matter of course, and familial pride, women and girls in Alcott's class were expected to spend most of their time inside these "pure," private homes directing their energies toward family and charity work, while men and boys charged outside into the fray of enterprise and politics. But even as a youngster, Louisa May Alcott did not fit this bifurcating cultural mold; nor was she willing to shape herself according to its outlines. Among a series of residential moves precipitated by her father's unpredictable finances and social experimentations, Louisa spent years in the storybook rural village of Concord, Massachusetts, with its temperate woods, glistening ponds, and fragrant gardens. As a child growing up in the 1830s and 1840s, Louisa would yank on her father's boots, burst through the doors of her cottage home, and tear across the high fields of the New England countryside. Stories of her nature walks and muddied skirts, told on tours at Orchard House, a museum in the Alcott family's former home in Concord and pictured in the 2019 film adaptation of her classic semi-autobiographical novel, *Little Women*, portray her youthful zest for adventure and her impatience with nineteenth-century gender norms. "I always thought I must have been a deer or a horse in some former state, because it was such a joy to run," Alcott revealed in a biographical essay. "No boy could be my friend till I had beaten him in a race, and no girl if she refused to climb trees, leap fences and be a tomboy," she boasted. Alcott relished pumping her legs and pushing her body to its limits, so much so that she identified with nonhuman animals *and* human boys, whose freedom to shape their quests and make their marks was intrinsically linked to spaces outside the home. Ironically, Louisa May Alcott would manage to carve out a singular space for herself in public and commercial life by capturing the idealized essence of the feminine New England household even as she undercut its meaning on the pages of her best-selling novel, *Little Women*.

If *Little Women* was a story built on Alcott's intimate understanding of feminine cultural mores tied to domestic space, it was also a tale inspired by Alcott's deep-seated desire to escape that very same form of enclosure. As a small child, Louisa acted on this impulse by repeatedly absconding from home. She started running away in Boston, where the Alcott family lived during her youngest years. Louisa confessed in retrospect and good humor that "running away was one of the delights of my childhood." One autumn day, after Louisa had just donned a "pretty little white dress with red dots," "red shoes," and had a "big red bow" tied in her hair by her mother, she bolted with no explanation to her caregivers. We might wonder if Louisa escaped in protest of the feminine outfit that was normative for girls of her race and social class in the 1830s. Clothing for girls—dresses, skirts, and undergarments—were traditionally wraparound pieces, while split-legged garments (pants) allowed boys much greater freedom of movement. Besides being annoyingly "cumbersome," girls' apparel was downright dangerous. "Long skirts collected debris from the streets, could weigh up to 25 pounds, and easily tripped a girl as she walked upstairs," the authors of a material history of girlhood wrote. Hence, "[a] girl's clothing was literally hazardous." In a biographical piece titled "Little Red Shoes," the writer Harriet Hobson attributes Louisa May Alcott's impulsive flight to wanting "to see the world." In this version of the oft-told story from Alcott's childhood, Louisa was out exploring, and apparently rebelling against her girlish dress, when the "bright day" turned gray as a storm broke. Alone and on foot in the rain, Louisa became disoriented, taking shelter in a doorway until her father found her late that evening.

The storm incident was not even the worst of Louisa May Alcott's early escapes. She frequently took to the Boston streets, "rolling her hoop on the Boston Common and then wandering away from home." On one occasion, Alcott, a self-described "weary little wanderer," wound up asleep on a stranger's doorstep with her head cushioned in the fur of a massive Newfoundland dog. The town crier discovered her at 9 p.m. that evening and returned her to her family. Louisa's mother, Abba Alcott, later tied her to the sofa to keep her from wandering off, literally tethering the child to feminized domestic space. Most memorable to Louisa—recounted at the beginning of her own autobiographical essay, second only to describing her earliest memories of books, her "greatest comfort"—was the time that she rolled her hoop to Boston Common and plunged into Frog Pond. She might have drowned had she not, as she succinctly reported, been "rescued by a black boy." Alcott writes that she became "a friend to the colored race then and there." This city pond once used for watering cattle in colonial Boston was the scene of her origin story for political awakening as an abolitionist. Her mother dated Louisa's antislavery orientation even earlier, calling her an abolitionist from the age of three.

While venturing outside alone and in the company of others, the young Louisa May Alcott preferred to engage in so-called masculine behaviors. According to one of her biographers, Susan Cheever, Alcott "act[ed] whenever she could as if she had been born a boy. She climbed trees, ran and jumped, and took dares. . . . She loved all animals, especially spiders, those creepy crawly creatures that make most girls scream." A journalist who characterized Alcott's childhood in a 1912 profile noted her passion for the outdoors, robust play, and writing, noting: "An outdoor life had given her a rugged constitution—she used to say she would not have a playmate who could not climb a tree. . . . 'I can't do much with my hands,' she wrote in her journal about this time, 'so I will use my head as a battering ram to make my way through this rough and tumble world.'" Alcott's father said of her in a speech: "In her young days, she would challenge any of the boys to feats of jumping, climbing, running, &c., and come off the victor." And Alcott herself disclosed that her "favorite retreat" as a girl in Concord was "an old cart-wheel, half hidden in grass under the locusts."

Alcott loved the unfettered space of the outdoors as well as the company of boys, but she was growing up in a culture that assigned the playroom and parlor to girls and the field and stream to boys. The world outside fed Louisa's imagination, even as her writing reflected the pleasures of outdoor life and the tensions of a culturally incongruent gender identity. The outdoors may have represented all that Alcott should not wish to be—wild and boyish. Alcott said in an interview very late in life: "I have often thought I may have been a horse before I was Louisa May Alcott. As a long-limbed child I had all a horse's delight in racing through the fields, and tossing my head to sniff the morning air. Now I am more than half-persuaded that I am a man's soul, put by some freak of nature into a woman's body." Attempting to label Alcott's gender identity with contemporary terminology would surely miss the mark and therefore misrepresent how she understood herself. Alcott probably felt like a "tomboy," in the meaning of that term in her time (which was not associated with cultural deviance or sexuality), and in more expansive ways that she may not have had the language for. As a teenager, Louisa knew that her gender tendencies made her unusual, once writing in her journal, "People think I'm wild and queer." She consistently associated her

"female masculinity" with outdoor space and wildness. It was outdoors and, she fantasized, in another corporeal form (the horse, the
deer, the boy) that Louisa May Alcott could fully be herself.

The young Louisa made a habit of traversing the gardens, parks,
streets, and woods near her family's various homes in the city and
the countryside. When, in 1840, the Alcotts moved from Boston
to the rural hamlet of Concord, eight-year-old Louisa devoted time
to tending the abundant household garden. Bronson Alcott proudly
grew carrots, peas, potatoes, parsnips, pears, melons, cucumbers,
spinach, squash, leeks, tomatoes, onions, beets, pumpkins, grapes,
and blackberries and welcomed his daughters' contributions. In an
1846 diary, Louisa May Alcott's sister, Elizabeth "Lizzie" Alcott,
recorded running "about the garden with Louisa" and weeding potatoes with her. The garden was situated on the safe cultural border
between domestic and untamed spaces as a cultivated and relatively
controlled slice of the outdoors.

But Louisa also explored the forests and fields of Concord with
her mother's indulgence. She later praised her mother's wisdom in
"turn[ing] me loose in the country and let[ting] me run wild, learning of nature what no books can teach." Highlighting one moment
in which she felt a spiritual awe awakened by natural beauty, Alcott
described coming to a sense of the sublime, or God revealed in
nature: "I remember running over the hills just at dawn one summer
morning, and pausing to rest in the silent woods saw, through an
arch of trees, the sun rise over river, hill and wide green meadows
as I never saw it before. Something born of the lovely hour, a happy
mood, and the unfolding aspirations of a child's soul seemed to bring
me very near to God." As an adult, Alcott described "those Concord
days" as the "happiest in [her] life."

Although Louisa May Alcott does not mention it in her reminiscences, Concord, like Boston, was a multiracial village. Built on
land formerly belonging to Nipmuc and Massachusett people, most
of whom had relocated due to colonial violence and economic hardships that displaced many Native people in the Massachusetts Bay
Colony a century prior, Concord was a settlement where a girl like
Louisa May Alcott would encounter people who were Indigenous
and Black. The woods surrounding Walden Pond were inhospita-
ble to farming and transit, and because formerly enslaved people in

*This photograph shown on a postcard is most likely of the home and farm where Louisa
May Alcott lived as a child growing up in Concord, Massachusetts. The back of the
postcard reads: "House where May Alcott was born – Concord, Mass. USA, Sept. 2,
1870." The image bears a likeness to a drawing of the family home made by Bronson
Alcott in a letter to his daughter.* Louisa May Alcott Papers, Courtesy of Houghton Library,
Harvard University.

Concord were only afforded undesirable land after the Revolutionary
War (a new state constitution ended slavery in the 1780s), many settled there. Walden Pond was in many ways a multiracial landscape
in the 1850s when transcendentalist Henry David Thoreau first published *Walden; or, Life in the Woods* (1854).

Louisa May Alcott fondly recalled hours spent outside in this
area, described as "black space" by a historian of slavery in Concord,
with her sisters and neighbor, Thoreau. She would glide in Thoreau's
rowboat across Walden Pond, take long walks with the writer, and
listen to his thoughts about nature, and possibly about Black history,
as Thoreau had devoted most of a chapter to the topic in *Walden*. For
Alcott, the ponds and groves of Massachusetts were spaces beyond
the limits of Victorian parlor society, where a teenaged Anglo-
American girl could while away the hours with a grown (not yet
famous) male philosopher and pass by the places where descendants
of enslaved African Americans and Native Americans had made
their homes. By plunging outside, seizing the "rough and tumble" of
life, and circumventing gender norms, Louisa May Alcott found a
unique authorial voice. That voice, and her representation of a young,
imperfect "tomboy" protagonist, would make Alcott one of America's first and most celebrated authors for children and young adults.

Because of her high energy level, Louisa's parents sent her back
to Boston to stay with her grandfather before the birth of her youngest sister, Abigail May. Bronson Alcott wrote a charming letter to
his daughter to ease her loneliness. The note, feelingly rendered and
touchingly illustrated, highlights Louisa's bold, outdoorsy personality and reveals her father's paternal affection as well as his disap-
proval. Bronson Alcott opens the letter to his exiled daughter in a
playful tone, saying: "We all miss the noisy girl who used to make

house and garden, barn and field ring with her footsteps, and even the hens and chickens seem to miss her too. Right glad would Father and Mother, Anna and Elisabeth . . . the House Play-room, Dolls, Hoop, Garden, Flowers, Fields, Woods and Brooks, all be to see and answer the voice and footsteps, the eye and hand, of their little companion." Then Bronson Alcott's words turn implicitly critical. "But yet all make themselves happy and beautiful without her; all seem to say, "Be good, little Miss, while away from us." He ends the letter with: "Be good, kind, gentle, while you are away, step lightly, and speak soft about the house." While clearly fond of Louisa, Bronson Alcott instructs her to behave like a proper girl. Her grandfather, who "loves quiet," should barely know she is there, as it was the consensus view of their social class that girls should be seen but not heard.

Perhaps the admonition to be quiet influenced Louisa May Alcott's penchant for the pen. She kept a journal, wrote stories, and began to publish action-packed romantic thrillers under a pseudonym as a young woman in Boston. In 1860, Alcott saw Harriet Tubman dramatize her experiences as an Underground Railroad activist at a fundraiser in the city. And it is possible that Alcott saw Tubman in an even more intimate setting a year prior, as Harriet Tubman spent days in Concord in the spring of 1859, visiting with the Alcott family among others in the town's antislavery circle. Soon after hearing Tubman in Boston, Alcott, who was by then in her late twenties, published two short stories with abolitionist and integrationist themes. The eruption of the Civil War in 1861 heightened Louisa May Alcott's sense of patriotic duty. At the age of thirty, she traveled to Washington, DC, to serve as a Union nurse, an experience that led her to publish the popular 1863 book *Hospital Sketches*.

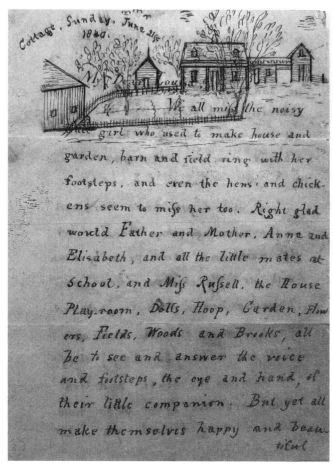

Bronson Alcott wrote this illustrated letter to his daughter, Louisa May
Alcott, while she was staying with her grandfather in Boston, June 21, 1840.
Courtesy of Houghton Library, Harvard University.

In 1868, seven years after Harriet Jacobs's *Incidents in the Life of
a Slave Girl* was published, the first volume of Louisa May Alcott's
classic novel—*Little Women: Meg, Jo, Beth, and Amy, The Story of Their
Lives, A Girls' Book*—appeared on the bookshop shelves. Loosely
based on members of her own family and on experiences of her

childhood in Concord, *Little Women* featured four close-knit sisters living in a loving, Christian home during the Civil War. While Jacobs had focused on a nightmare domestic scenario in which a teenaged girl was trapped by a man who also professed the Christian faith, Alcott focused on a cheerful, idealized domestic sphere modeled on Orchard House, her family's home in Concord from the late 1850s to the 1870s, where she had written the book in just four months. *Little Women* won Alcott acclaim, wealth, and thousands of instant fans.

Into this sweet story about proper girlhood, family ties, and Christian values, Louisa May Alcott smuggled a different gender sensibility—a tomboy sensibility—by way of the main character who was beloved by readers. The figure of the "tomboy," the fun-loving, comedic Anglo-American girl who climbed trees, whistled, and complained about skirts, had begun appearing in American print early in the nineteenth century. But none of those previous heroines was as fully fleshed out, independent, and intellectual as the singular Jo March. "Alcott did something more with Jo," one literature scholar writes: "This tomboy was not simply funny and winsome, but smart, ambitious, and more comfortable defying feminine convention than trying to live up to its demands." By creating a girl who refused ladylike restrictions and dared to rebuff the eventual marriage proposal of her childhood best friend, Louisa May Alcott scripted a gender rebel into American fiction in the period when popular women's fiction had elevated sentimentality, domesticity, and femininity.

Louisa May Alcott's Jo March was a revolutionary character and proto-feminist figure in mid-nineteenth-century America. But Alcott's biographers have noted the bittersweet contradiction that in Jo March, Louisa May Alcott created the character that she could not be—or remain—in real life. John Mattheson writes that Alcott "wanted to express herself—or, more accurately, the self she remembered being in her youth—frankly on the page. Through Jo, she wanted to present her own spirit, with neither the veneer of tact nor the gloss of propriety." And Susan Cheever shows that Alcott created in Jo March a girl who "shared her love of apples and cats and who, miraculously, was beloved even though she was a rebel."

Louisa May Alcott projected her own feelings and desires onto Jo, the protagonist of *Little Women* and a middle sister in the intensely moralizing, self-sacrificing March family. It is through this character that Alcott's own enjoyment of the outdoors and of boys' pursuits is most clearly expressed. In Alcott's portrayal, Jo March is a fiercely fun, physically active, ambitious girl "whose greatest affliction" lay "in the fact that she couldn't read, run, and ride as much as she liked." Readers quickly learn that "a quick temper, sharp tongue, and restless spirit were always getting [Jo] into scrapes, and her life was a series of ups and downs, which were both comic and pathetic." Jo is pronounced unfeminine immediately in the novel. In the opening scene she "examine[s] her boots in a gentlemanly manner," according to the narrator, and whistles in a "boyish" way in the view of her sister Amy. Although Jo's eldest sister, Meg, tells her to "leave off boyish tricks" and to "remember that you are a young lady," Jo resists. "I hate to think I've got to grow up, and be Miss March, and wear long gowns, and look as prim as a China aster," she protests to her sisters. "It's bad enough to be a girl, anyway, when I like boys' games and work and manners. I can't get over my disappointment at not being a boy." The gentle sister of the novel, Beth, speaks up to soothe Jo, whose full name is Josephine: "Poor Jo; it's too bad! But it can't be helped, so you must try to be contented with making your name boyish, and playing brother to us girls."

But Jo is *not* contented. She declares herself "the man of the family" while her father is away serving as a chaplain for the Union army and acts the male parts when her siblings put on plays. Before a New Year's Eve party at the home of a wealthy neighbor, Jo fails to curl her hair and accidentally burns her dress in the fireplace. The dress, perhaps like Jo's forced femininity, is "nicely mended" but still shows scorch marks. Jo meets her new best friend, Theodore (Laurie) Laurence, during the party, but their relationship requires the outdoors to mature. The relatively unrestrictive natural world better accommodates the mismatched friendship of a retiring rich boy and financially insecure boyish girl. They play chase in the garden, much to Jo's sister's shock. And throughout the dreamy weeks of summer, Jo spends her days "on the river with Laurie" and reading "up in the apple tree," enjoying the gender flexibility that natural surroundings and lesser surveillance afford. Unlike the author who created her, the character Jo March has license to express her feelings about gender identification, to roughhouse with a best boyfriend, and to flout feminine conventions. What is more, the doting fictional father seems to accept this identity, referring to his child as "son Jo" after returning from the battlefield.

Even as Louisa May Alcott created a feisty protagonist whose words and actions illuminated the suppressive nature of gender constraint that girls faced, she was compelled to compromise Jo's character arc and the story's plotline. Jo March was adored by her family, but she was also scrutinized and criticized by them. Her vigorous romp in the garden with Laurie was witnessed by her sister Meg, who proclaimed judgmentally, in the choral voice of society, that Jo would never "behave like a young lady." And Jo's father, who joked that she was like a son, noticed a change in her after his return from war service. "I don't see the 'son Jo' whom I left a year ago," the character Robert March observed. "I see a young lady who pins her collar straight, laces her boots neatly, and neither whistles, talks slang, nor lies on the rug as she used to do. . . . I rather miss my wild girl, but if I get a strong, helpful, tenderhearted woman in her place, I shall feel quite satisfied." Robert March conveys a message like Bronson Alcott's in his letter to Louisa: while the wild unfeminine child was beloved and even missed by her father, she must be supplanted by a self-restrained young lady. The character Jo had matured from a tree-climbing, freewheeling colt-like girl into a proper "little woman."

Alcott's readership, made up chiefly of white girls and young women with means, would hold their favorite author to account regarding representations of girlhood, womanhood, and cultural mores. When Alcott did not marry Jo and Laurie at the end of volume 1 of *Little Women*, she received a barrage of pleadings to wed the couple in the next installment. Alcott, who was in her thirties when the book came out, had not herself married. She resisted attaching her semi-autobiographical protagonist to a spouse, swearing in her journal: "I won't marry Jo to Laurie to please any one." Yet, with the pressure of her publisher added to her readers' professed wish, Alcott recognized the commercial necessity of a romantic plotline. While she refused to give in fully to audience desires and cultural dictates by pairing Jo with Laurie, she did finally include a marriage between Jo and a brooding professor, striking a delicate balance between competing visions of women's possibilities. *Little Women* was the first in a trilogy of popular novels about the March family, followed by *Little Men* (1871) and *Jo's Boys* (1886), catapulting Louisa May Alcott into celebrity and wide acclaim as "a beloved mentor and writer for young girls."

In her fifties, Louisa May Alcott became a mother, adopting the infant daughter of her deceased sister, the artist May Alcott Nieriker. Alcott championed women's equality, attended suffrage meetings, wrote essays in support of women's rights, and became the first woman registered to vote in Concord. Alcott chose an adult life that kept her single, in charge of her own career and finances, and sexually independent. She once indicated erotic feelings for women, telling an interviewer: "I have fallen in love in my life with so many pretty girls, and never once the least little bit with any man." She claimed for herself the autonomy of white, middle-class manhood, even as she devoted significant time and funds to the care of family members and maintained a feminine personal aesthetic, appearing in photographs in the "Gilded age finery" of velvets, ruffles, and lace. Perhaps the mature Louisa May Alcott no longer felt the desire to wear male costumes and take to the woods like her character Jo March, or perhaps she suppressed such urges or concealed them in the privacy of her own home. Nonetheless, Alcott's insistence on living out womanhood differently and her imagining of a new kind of American heroine began with her bold activities as a girl outdoors. In her classic work, Louisa May Alcott pushed the cultural needle toward recognition and acceptance of a broader range of gender expression for girls and the adults they would become. Through her intimate relationship with outdoor places, Louisa May Alcott became a "nature" writer in more ways than one, revealing for her readership the restrictive nature of Victorian girlhood and the environmental aspects of gender ideology and social control.

If writing about nature became a subtle tool of social commentary for Louisa May Alcott, it served a similar purpose for a contemporary, a young Native American woman who would be called "the northern Pocahontas" by the American man she had married. Jane Johnston Schoolcraft was born Bamewawagezhikaquay, an Anishinaabe (Ojibwe) name that translates as "The Sound the Stars Make Rushing through the Sky." A daughter of Susan Johnston (Ozhaguscodaywayquay, or Green Prairie Woman) and the Scottish-Irish trader John Johnston (whom her mother had been forced to marry by her own father), Jane was born in 1800. She grew up along the shining St. Mary River near Lake Huron and played in the lush woods and crystal waters of Sault Ste. Marie, a town in the Great Lakes with a large Indigenous as well as French population. Her family was mixed-race and culturally nimble. She spoke at least two languages, Anishinaabemowin (Ojibwe) and English, and she would have been used to hearing French. Jane Johnston's parents expected her to marry a Euro-American man, as was by then common in Great Lakes fur trade culture. They raised her accordingly. Jane studied in her father's home library and traveled to Ireland with him, where she spent time with her aunt to further her learning before taking ill and returning to Michigan.

In 1823, Jane Johnston wed Henry Rowe Schoolcraft, an ambitious writer with an anthropological interest in Native American cultural practices and the first federal Indian agent in Michigan

Territory. Theirs has been called a "literary marriage," and indeed, it was. Jane Johnston Schoolcraft was a poet and short story writer and one of the earliest Native American women known to have published verse. Henry Rowe Schoolcraft became a respected writer and ethnographer. In the 1820s, he founded and edited a magazine called *The Literary Voyager*. In 1839, he published a book of intensively edited Great Lakes Native stories, including material he gleaned from his wife but failed to publicly attribute to her. That book, *Algic Researches*, inspired Henry Wadsworth Longfellow's famous (and unfortunately, stereotype-inducing) poem *The Song of Hiawatha*. It was by publishing in her husband's magazine and traveling to New York that Jane gained a modest readership as the "northern Pocahontas"—her husband's descriptor that resonated with the public's romanticization of Native American women's pasts, obscuring the harsher realities.

The mystique that prompted Henry Rowe Schoolcraft's use of the name Pocahontas was one that blurred two Indigenous female figures who became increasingly famous in nineteenth-century America, just as Native American populations were facing expulsion from their homelands: Pocahontas, who lived in the early 1600s, and Sacagawea (Sacajawea) lived in the early 1800s. Both women's biographies belie rosy interpretation. Pocahontas, whose Algonquian name translated to "Mischief" or "Little Playful One," or "Little Mischief" and who was also called Amonute and Matoaka by her family, was born to the Pamunkey people of the Powhatan Confederacy of present-day tidewater Virginia around 1595 or 1596.

Pocahontas was just eleven or twelve when English colonists arrived on her people's coast and built the historic settlement of Jamestown in 1607. Her father, Powhatan (Wahunsenacawh), was a paramount chief with political authority over several Indigenous towns, gained by intermarriage as well as warfare. When the English arrived, the powerful Powhatan had to determine how best to size up and interact with the newcomers, and he probably expected to pull this new settlement into the orbit of his political influence. He assigned Pocahontas, the one of his many children who seemed to have an especially outgoing, confident, and adventuresome personality, to the task of diplomacy. It was during this first year of encounter that Pocahontas may have ritually adopted Captain John Smith, an English leader, to seal a political alliance rendered in kinship terms at the behest of Powhatan. This event has been dramatized in American lore as Pocahontas throwing her body over Smith's to save him from death at her father's hand and thereby ultimately saving the future American nation. But scholars and tribal citizens agree that if this scene took place, it would not have been an act of passion performed at the whim of a single girl, but rather a community-sanctioned ritual. Pocahontas was later held captive by the English. She converted to Christianity soon after her confinement, married the slaveholding tobacco planter John Rolfe, had a son, and died during a trip to England around the age of twenty-one.

Pocahontas shares mythological space with Sacagawea, the Shoshone teenager who accompanied Captains Meriwether Lewis and William Clark as they traversed the continent with a military cadre in 1805–1806 at the direction of President Thomas Jefferson. Sacagawea traveled with the Corps of Discovery because her "husband" accepted a job as translator. Right before the trip

commenced, Sacagawea had given birth to a baby boy in a difficult delivery and then carried him in a cradleboard for hundreds of
miles with only men for company. Although she was instrumental
to the journey as a translator, forager, and the only person with consequential social ties and specific cultural knowledge, Sacagawea
was never compensated for her contributions. Numerous romantic
tales have been written about Pocahontas and Sacagawea, depicting
both as lovely Indian maidens or "princesses" who fell in love with
dashing English men (for Pocahontas, the entirely fabricated love
interest was Captain John Smith; for Sacagawea, Captain William
Clark) and along the way acted as sacrificial saviors of the American
colonial project to settle the lands and build a new Anglo society
(Pocahontas by "saving" John Smith; Sacagawea by "piloting" the
Lewis and Clark expedition).

Pocahontas and Sacagawea were first linked in American
nationalistic mythology by the white suffragist Eva Emery Dye, who
memorialized Sacagawea and compared her to Pocahontas in her
popular 1902 novel, *The Conquest: The True Story of Lewis and Clark.*
Dye thought that American expansion into Native territories was
right as well as inevitable, and she also believed that white women
should play a critical role in this enlarged American life through
voting rights. For Dye, who turned to the Lewis and Clark journals for source material and was instrumental to (but not credited
for) their later publication, Sacagawea could serve as an exemplar. In
Dye's fictional rendering, Sacagawea was maternal, domestic, and
helpful as she opened the gates to the West for Euro-American men.
Dye classed Sacagawea alongside Pocahontas as "the most trav-
elled Indian Princess in our history." And while Dye enlisted the
longstanding trope of the American Indian princess to promote her

political vision, she aggrandized Captains John Smith, Meriwether Lewis, and William Clark by referring to them as demigod-like "immortals." Together, the romanticized versions of Sacagawea and Pocahontas affirmed the value of welcoming, feminized womanhood to the American nation and justified the acquisition of Indigenous lands, which these women's actions of "saving" and "leading" the colonizers seemed to sanction. Imagined as representing the land itself, Indigenous women were seen as symbolically giving up acreage when they supposedly gave their bodies to couple with white men. This disturbing mythology, which turns on an objectification of Indigenous women and on a feminization of "new" lands, pretends that Indigenous people were willing to be displaced and that Native women welcomed and willfully aided that ultimately violent and deadly process of dispossession.

Eva Emery Dye, a midwesterner by birth who had moved to Oregon with her husband, was among a group of Euro-American women who raised funds to commission a statue to their version of Sacagawea. At the celebratory unveiling in Portland, well-known suffragists Susan B. Anthony and Anna Howard Shaw spoke to the crowd. Shaw's comments portrayed Sacagawea as a "forerunner" for women's suffrage, albeit one whose "tribe" was "fast disappearing," in keeping with another popular nineteenth-century trope—the vanishing Indian. In Shaw's view, Sacagawea provided the country with a model of "calm endurance, of patient persistence and unfaltering courage," but since her people were fated to fade into history, winning the vote would not include them.

Native American women activists had a different perspective on the longevity of their people in the places they called home, and they voiced their views in the same historical moment when some prominent suffragists tried to relegate them to a misty past by harkening back to Sacagawea and Pocahontas. The Dakota writer Gertrude Simmons Bonnin (who later adopted the Lakota language pen name Zitkála-Šá), was an advocate for Native rights and women's rights. As a college student in Indiana, Bonnin earned the honor of competing in a statewide speech competition. Before a large audience of other students in the state capitol of Indianapolis in 1896, Bonnin represented Earlham College, offering a speech titled "Side by Side" that argued for interracial respect. She was the only woman, as well as the only Native American, to speak in the contest. After giving her remarks, Bonnin watched a group of attendees display a banner picturing a caricatured Indian girl and the racial slur "sq—". Bonnin described this incident as an example of "strong prejudice against my people," a "barbarian rudeness" that caused her to feel "embittered." Although she was incensed, Bonnin felt vindicated when she took second prize at the oratory contest.

As Gertrude Bonnin's career developed, she stood among many women of color who spoke out or demonstrated to advance suffrage. While Bonnin took to the stage, others organized and marched, asserting not only political rights, but also physical rights to occupy public space. Among these protestors was the Chinese American teenager Mabel Lee, who was only sixteen when she rode on horseback at the front of the New York suffrage parade in 1912, the most spectacular gathering of women's rights advocates in the country up to that time. The African American journalist Ida B. Wells, who had exposed the rampant crime of lynching, organized a suffrage club and marched in a Washington, DC, suffrage parade in 1913. And Anna Julia Cooper, a Black graduate of Oberlin College who earned her doctorate in Paris, pursued women's rights through education indoors and out. In 1892, Cooper published a manifesto, *A Voice from the South*, that championed women's accomplishments across time and cultures and advocated for Black women's dignity, and in 1911–1912, she founded what may have been the first African American–led girls' outdoor club. While serving as a teacher of classics in Washington, DC, Cooper established the original chapter of the YWCA's Camp Fire Girls, a group that visited natural areas to camp and swim. By 1921, Cooper had 618 girls enrolled in her outdoor program—one year after "women" secured the vote in the Nineteenth Amendment to the Constitution, but three years before Native Americans nominally did in the Indian Citizenship Act of 1924 and decades before Black Southern women did in the Voting Rights Act of 1965.

During the suffrage movement, women from diverse backgrounds took to the streets, claiming public, outdoor space for political ends. This photograph captures a scene from a suffrage parade in New York City in which participants held up banners and wore academic robes. Photo by Jessie Tarbox Beals, 1910. Used by permission of the Schlesinger Library, Harvard Radcliffe Institute, Harvard University.

Jane Johnston Schoolcraft was no "Pocahontas" in the rose-tinted sense that Henry Rowe Schoolcraft intended in the 1830s. Neither was Pocahontas herself, or Sacagawea, or any of the prominent and politically active Native women who followed in their footsteps over the centuries. But Jane Johnston Schoolcraft was indeed a child of an Indigenous eastern woodland community. This was an aspect of her background that worried her husband. While Henry liked to emphasize his wife's descendancy from "one of the highest and proudest circles of Irish society," he was frustrated by her lack of enthusiasm for living as a Christian wife and blamed this on her upbringing "in a remote place . . . without the salutary influence of society." In other words, he had concerns about the purported wildness of Jane's youth preventing her from achieving full acculturation in an American home over which he was head.

In contrast, Jane Johnston Schoolcraft praised the place where she was born, devoting loving, literary attention to the azure rivulets and emerald leaves of the interior Great Lakes, while sharing her cultural knowledge, communal attachment, and subtle political critiques. Descriptions of natural features and her rush of feelings about them abound in her writing. In the poem "Lines Written at Castle Island, Lake Superior," Jane relates: "Here in my native inland sea . . . How wide, how sweet, how fresh and free." She concludes this verse with these telling lines: "Far from the haunts of men away / For here, there are no sordid fears, No crimes, no misery, no tears / No pride of wealth; the heart to fill / No laws to treat my people ill." Jane does not directly comment on the fact that her own husband was charged with enforcing American law as the regional Indian agent, but surely this political awareness, and the uncomfortable realities of colonial intimacies, teemed behind her words. Jane Johnston Schoolcraft often wrote about the lakes and inscribed odes to trees. Her poem "To the Pine Tree," which she wrote in Anishinaabemowin after her trip to Europe, is a striking example. A translation reads: "The pine! The pine! I eager cried / The pine, my father! See it stand / As first that cherished tree I spied / Returning to my native land." Jane claims the pine tree as a paternal relative in this stanza and later refers to "my own dear bright mother land." To her, the land and its features are kin held dear in relationships both expressed and enacted. In the poem "On the Doric Rock, Lake Superior," Jane describes the "simple Indian" who "Looks up to Nature's God above the skies / And though, his lot be rugged wild and dear / Yet owns the ruling power with soul sincere." Here she intentionally calls to mind romantic American notions of the untutored "wild" Indian in order to assert an alternative perspective: wildness is next to godliness, a contemplative state of being. It is the Native person, viewed as "simple" by American society, who not only knows how to tap into true power seated in the natural world, but also owns this knowledge.

Jane Johnston Schoolcraft quietly proclaimed fealty to her homeland, a place representative of wild freedom, through nature poetry. Her lyrical expressions of reverence were at the same time claims of community belonging and Indigenous sovereignty, the right to political and cultural self-determination, embedded in the landscape and waterscape of the people. She does not speak in the voice of a Native woman who willingly gives up land and water or her own body and emotions, like the mythical Indian princesses of American lore. Instead, her writings on nature are shot through with the realism of separation, denigration, and the changes time and colonialism had wrought. Notably, Jane wrote her most intimate poems in her mother tongue, Anishinaabemowin. Henry Rowe Schoolcraft's translation, in which he took liberties, embellished her prose. But a modern translation by Anishinaabe language specialists offers a streamlined iteration of one of Jane's most haunting poems that captures the spare beauty of her thought and craftswomanship. Jane penned the untitled verse after relinquishing her children to eastern boarding schools, most likely at her husband's insistence. It includes lines addressed to "My little daughter" and "My little son" and promises "To my home I shall return / That is the way that I am, my being / My land." Jane Johnston Schoolcraft's lines convey love and loss on an intimate scale, together with an implicit criticism of American imposition and extraction. "Ahh but I am sad," reads the last line of this farewell song, which doubles as an homage to kin and home. Her potent words remain with us still, love poem and lament, carrying the sound the stars make rushing through the sky.

Mamie Garvin Fields, a Black girl who grew up a generation later than Alcott and Schoolcraft, split her time between the refined city of Charleston and rural South Carolina cotton fields. After a community-oriented career as a teacher and Black women's club organizer, Fields published her personal account of a Southern upbringing, *Lemon Swamp and Other Places: A Carolina Memoir*, in collaboration with her granddaughters, Karen and Barbara Fields, in 1983. Born in 1888, the year of Louisa May Alcott's premature death, Mamie Garvin Fields was raised as a relatively privileged African American girl in the post-Reconstruction and Progressive era South of the 1880s and 1890s. She spent leisure time on a family farm at Lemon Swamp, a place of sweet and bitter memories where her grandmother "was lost."

As an adult storyteller recalling her childhood, Fields voiced ambivalence about Lemon Swamp, which had been the scene of captivity and freedom, diminishment and daring, love and loss over the course of her family's history. Mamie's grandfather had once been enslaved on a cotton plantation at the site. After his owners ran out of fear of General William Tecumseh Sherman's troops during the Civil War, Mamie's Grandpa Hannibal remained on the grounds. By squatting there, he assumed informal "ownership" of the remote place, which the family referred to as a farm rather than a plantation, obscuring its ugly roots through their choice of language, as Mamie realizes when she tells the story to her granddaughters decades later. Mamie traveled to Lemon Swamp with her family each summer, delighting in the relaxed rhythms and wild surrounds. Lemon Swamp shimmered as a special place in her memory. "All kinds of wild things grew in Lemon Swamp," she recalled, "tall, sweet-smelling pine trees, huge live oaks that touched one another over the road, ferns of every shape growing close to the water, other plants growing right in the water." There she watched birds "that you could never see anywhere else," observed "little animals," and enjoyed the way the cool swamp enclosed her as if a "room," where "trees and bushes threw shadows . . . like the curtains." Here was a world of "strange places and secret hideouts," the refuge and rejoinder for an agile-minded African American child.

While this secluded pool transfixed the young Mamie, it was a painful place for her grandfather, who cried as he told the story of losing his wife at the swamp when their owner took her away to serve the mistress and white children. This was a story her grandfather told her always through tears. The legal owner of her grandparents, Mr. Garvin, heard Sherman's soldiers were on the way and ordered the self-exile of his family and the Black people they owned, who helped to transport "the best furniture, the good dishes, his silver and his gold." As the party wound clandestinely through Lemon Swamp, Garvin decided to divide them, sending Mamie's grandfather and children to hide a stash of food but commanding Mamie's grandmother to remain with the white family. As the child nurse, she was directed to tend Mrs. Garvin's four children: "a breast child, a lap child, a floor child, and a walker." Mamie's grandfather "begged the master not to take his wife." Garvin refused to relent, prioritizing his own family's comfort. "Not a word ever came back from the owner and his wife, or from Grandma," Mamie Garvin Fields concludes. "My grandmother was lost in Lemon Swamp and was never seen again." The American Civil War that had divided the nation over the institution of slavery had shattered Mamie's own family. Yet it also resulted in her grandfather's emancipation and his attainment of the very land that held the bog she loved.

Mamie Garvin Fields withholds this disclosure of horror at the swamp until the final moment of her telling, perhaps reluctant to tarnish her golden memory of the place or to cast the site and the book named for it beneath the existential shadow of slavery. "So that was Lemon Swamp," Fields says, at last, in summary. "If it was a beautiful, secret room in the daytime, it was the Boogeyman's pit at night." Memory, for this young daughter of enslaved grandparents, is yoked to outdoor spaces with complex intergenerational meanings. In her poignant recollection of the emotional contradictions that can be embedded in beloved places, Mamie Garvin Fields reflects Toni Morrison's famous insight about the temporal and natural movement of memory. Writers are like floodwaters, Morrison lyrically relates, "remembering where we were, what valley we ran through, what the banks were like, the light that was there and the route back to our original place." Wordsmiths are not only observers of nature in Morrison's recasting; they are akin to nature's elemental forces in returning essential memories to us. Writers flood the canyon walls of our cultures, flushing and remaking our corporate shapes. It is apt and not coincidental that Toni Morrison crafted this waterborne analogy, for she holds a place in the underground tradition of Black women nature writers that includes the poet Audre Lorde as a contemporary and Mamie Garvin Fields, as well as Harriet Jacobs, as literary ancestors.

Across geographical, racial, and ethnic distances, the brooding yet beautiful Lemon Swamp, the wild but endangered Lake Superior, and the placid yet dangerous Frog Pond shaped the lives and imaginations of Mamie Garvin Fields, Jane Johnston Schoolcraft, and Louisa May Alcott. These waters prove transformative in the women's recollections. Frog Pond was the place where Alcott "became" an abolitionist, or at least developed an early consciousness of a racial divide with gendered aspects that privileged the protection of white girls. Lake Superior was the source for Jane Johnston Schoolcraft's declaration of an Indigenous form of spiritual understanding that could survive the influx of American encroachment. And Lemon Swamp was the place where Mamie Garvin Fields first grasped a family history of racial terror that would haunt but also politicize her. These women writers who spent uncountable childhood hours outdoors returned to meaningfully ambivalent places on the page, flooding the valley of the past with reflective light and washing new visions onto the banks of the future.

CHAPTER 3

GAME CHANGERS

———

"GIVE THE GIRLS a chance!" Anna Julia Cooper demanded in her bold book, *A Voice from the South*. "We might as well expect to grow trees from leaves as hope to build up a civilization or a manhood without taking into consideration our women and the home life made for them." In 1892, when her monograph was published, Cooper, a teacher and formerly enslaved child of an enslaved Black woman and the man that owned them both, was speaking to Black ministers, intellectuals, institution builders, churchwomen, and club women as well as to white suffragists at a time when the education of women was not a given and the vote for women had not been secured. She appealed to her readers by making the pitch that an educated Black girl could ultimately uplift her family, improve Black homes, and better the race. And indeed, she believed this, just as she believed that prominent women's rights advocates like Anna Howard Shaw should stop making comments on the public stage that minimized the struggles of American Indians. "All prejudices, whether of race, sect or sex, class pride and caste distinctions, are the belittling inheritance and badge of snobs and prigs," Cooper warned. And Cooper believed, too, that educating African American girls was transportive for their inner beings. Through "intellectual development," Cooper insisted, "her horizon is extended. Her sympathies are broadened and deepened and multiplied. She is in closer touch with nature. Not a bud that opens, not a dew drop, not a ray of light, not a cloud-burst or a thunderbolt, but adds to the expansiveness and zest of her soul." With an educated mind, Anna Julia Cooper suggested, a girl can better appreciate the wonders of nature and her place in it. This may have been true for African Americans attending school by choice, but Cooper could not have imagined the cumulative heartache that forced education would bring to Native American girls.

While a young Anna Julia Cooper studied in a Raleigh, North Carolina, school for formerly enslaved people in the Reconstruction era of the 1870s, a strict federal education system aimed at Native American children was taking shape in Pennsylvania and would soon spread to the western states. The education of Native American children in European institutions had a long history in the country, stretching back to independent programs at early religious colleges like Harvard and Dartmouth in the colonial period and to missionary schools supported by churches, donors, and government contributions in the early nineteenth century. But the federal Indian boarding school took these prototypes to extremes, introducing a network of carceral institutions that removed Indigenous children from their communities in the name of education.

By the 1890s, when Cooper published her book, a girl named Genevieve Healy was among the approximately twenty thousand Indigenous youths who attended a federal boarding school during the late nineteenth and early twentieth centuries. Genevieve was born around 1888, the same period that the federal government pushed her people, the Aaniiih (Gros Ventre), onto what became known as the Fort Belknap Indian Reservation, bordered by the Milk River in northern Montana. While reservations were coerced enclosures resented by many Native American elders, for children who had never known or barely recalled a pre-reservation era of independent mobility, these mandated areas became home. Genevieve Healy spent her first years surrounded by kin on Fort Belknap, a land of craggy stone buttes where mottled rattlesnakes sunned, spring-fed creeks cut through the prairie, and winking deposits of pure gold lay beneath the Little Rocky Mountains. She loved her home in the snug community of Lodge Pole, tucked up against the foothills where the mountains met the plains. Nevertheless, she would find herself transported halfway across the state to the military-style brick complex that composed a new government boarding school. In the 1890s, the same decade that Genevieve moved far away from Fort Belknap and residents there were pressured by government representatives into signing away their sacred mountains so gold could be mined, a sport invented in Massachusetts to keep students active during the winter would also travel to that distant complex called Fort Shaw.

As a matter of feeling and maybe principle, Genevieve Healy did not like school—or at least the rigid, stingy schooling that was supplied for her and her tribal classmates. Genevieve was a physically active, outspoken child who "preferred riding across the open range to sounding out letters in a classroom where she was obliged to hold her tongue, [and] speak only in English." She relished outdoor activity and experienced school as a "prison," her granddaughter, Donita Nordlund, told the interviewers Linda Peavy and Ursula Smith in the early 2000s. This was a feeling Genevieve shared in common with Gertrude Bonnin (whose pen name was Zitkála-Šá, or "Red Bird" in English), the Dakota student who left her home reservation to attend a Quaker school contracted by the federal government in the 1880s and would later become a public speaker, author, and advocate for Native and women's rights. Having grown up on the Yankton Sioux Reservation in South Dakota in the 1870s–1880s, Bonnin described her girlhood and educational experiences in an essay collection, *American Indian Stories*, first published in 1921. Zitkála-Šá wrote of finding "joyous relief in running loose in the open" and "roam[ing] over the hills" with friends, held "in the lap of the prairie." Genevieve Healy seems to have felt much the same way.

But when Genevieve was around five years old, after her mother died in childbirth, her white father, a rancher who operated a trading post, succumbed to pressure from recruiters for federal boarding schools to send her and her siblings far away to be "educated." Despite the pain of separation from family, forced adherence to strict standards of comportment, and perhaps secret sources of pain that she did not share with her granddaughter (or her granddaughter did not disclose to interviewers), Healy survived and thrived. At Fort Shaw in the Sun River valley, an off-reservation boarding school, Genevieve Healy would join a team that set records for the modern sport called basketball and broke barriers for women athletes—an achievement made bittersweet by the racism against Indigenous people that she and her teammates experienced.

Major political upheavals in which the US government sought to take Indigenous lands formed the backdrop of Genevieve's attendance at two reservation schools and then her enrollment at Fort Shaw. In the mid to late 1800s, the United States forcibly relocated eighty thousand Cherokee, Chickasaw, Choctaw, Creek, Delaware,

Potawatomi, Shawnee, Seminole, and Seneca people from the Southeast and Midwest to Indian Territory of present-day Oklahoma and Kansas. Later in that period, the federal government, backed by state militias and vigilantes, used military might to coerce nations on the Great Plains, in the Rocky Mountains, in the Great Basin, and in the Southwest into treaties requiring Native tribes to reside on reserved lands—reservations—that would be held collectively and overseen by a federal government appointee known as the Indian agent.

Prior to the late 1800s, the Aaniiih people had moved through a region between the Saskatchewan and Missouri Rivers, crossing the northern plains and the not-always-existent Canadian-US border according to the season, living in select summer and winter villages, hunting buffalo as well as smaller game, and gathering plants and roots to supply their needs. At the time of Genevieve's birth, Fort Belknap residents of the Aaniiih (Gros Ventre) and Nakoda (Assiniboine) nations were struggling to adjust to the fixed boundaries and structurally imposed poverty of reservation life as well as to the depletion of the buffalo herds on which the people had depended for food, shelter, and clothing for generations.

With the establishment of the reservation and its federal surveillance apparatus came a Euro-American style of schooling. Rather than being traditionally educated in life skills, arts and crafts, and community beliefs and values by their family members, as well as by gifted storytellers who would gather listeners to tell the histories and sagas of their people, children at Fort Belknap were now expected to attend a private religious school or public government school on the reservation. Operated by Euro-American personnel, these local schools would teach the English language, inculcate Christian beliefs, and introduce basic academic subjects such as reading, spelling, and arithmetic. Catholic missionaries established St. Paul's Mission Church in 1887 and started a school the following year. Soon after, a government school opened at the Fort Belknap Agency (the most "developed" portion of the reservation, where the federally assigned US Indian agent had his office and managed the affairs of the tribes). Fort Belknap's reservation schools were intended to reshape Native life. Even as local schools made inroads toward "civilizing" Indigenous peoples, a complex new system of off-reservation boarding schools founded, sponsored, and administered by the federal Office of Indian Affairs had sweeping effects on Native children and their families.

At the first of these federal institutions, Carlisle Indian Industrial School in Pennsylvania, and the many other government boarding schools that would be built over the next three decades, students were expected to become adults who identified with the "Christian" values of dominant American society and thought of themselves as proto-citizens—embracing individualism, industriousness, personal property rights, nuclear households, and Euro-American gender roles with fixed notions of proper masculine and feminine behaviors. The caliber of citizenship imagined for Native Americans, however, would be different, as most Native people were not legal citizens of the United States and were not expected to enjoy a full menu of rights or to achieve middle-class economic status. Academic education at these schools would be introductory and rudimentary. Instead of studying advanced material, for instance, Native students would be trained in a plethora of manual skills that would suit them for agricultural and industrial labor, for work in white households, and for work in boarding schools. While government officials believed their educational policy was good for Native children and preferred to persuade parents to participate, agents often had to resort to manipulative and coercive measures to recruit attendees. These tactics included using trickery and partial truths to confuse parents and lure children, threatening to withhold food rations and annual treaty payments from families that did not comply, threatening physical force, and dispatching tribal police.

Not coincidentally, the mass removal of Native youth from their homes occurred during the prime years of adolescent development, when they would have matured into their tribal identities, learning, in the words of boarding school historians Brenda Child and Brian Klopotek, "what it means to be Ojibwe, Mohawk, or Hopi." Rather than preparing for adult membership and future leadership in their Indigenous communities in keeping with long-standing customs, at residential schools students learned to see those customs through different eyes—the eyes of educators who characterized Native ways as backward and uncivilized. The boarding school experiment, carried out roughly from the 1870s through the 1920s (and reformed in the 1930s), overlapped with the reservation era and continued into the allotment era that followed, in which the federal government sought to incorporate Native Americans into mainstream society, subdivide their common lands, and sell excess acreage resulting from this process to non-Native settlers and land speculators.

When Dr. William Winslow, head recruiter for Fort Shaw Indian School, Montana's new federal boarding school, visited Genevieve Healy's family ranch, he would have seen children playing freely and speaking in what to his ears may have sounded like a cacophonous mix of the Gros Ventre and French languages. A large family with several youngsters, a recently deceased Aaniiih mother, and a reliance on a French neighbor for childcare help, the Healys represented an opportunity for Winslow because of their multiple vulnerabilities. Colonel Healy at first refused to send his school-aged children away, but within a few years he would change his mind. In 1893, he sent Genevieve from the family ranch in Lodge Pole to an adjacent settlement called Hays to attend St. Paul's Mission School. The five-year-old Genevieve begged her father to bring her home, complaining, according to a paraphrased interview conducted with her granddaughter, that she had "never been so hungry, or so cold, or so miserable." William Healy then moved Genevieve and her siblings to the Fort Belknap Agency School, where Genevieve was also disheartened by the "cold and drafty dorm rooms, greasy food, and harsh discipline." Although she disliked the conditions and treatment at this second school as well, Genevieve made new friends, including an older Nakoda girl named Katie Snell. In 1895, Katie Snell's father, a white man who had served in the military as a scout and married an Assiniboine woman, and who had also been visited by Winslow, would agree to send Katie all the way to Fort Shaw. Genevieve's father sent her brother John to Fort Shaw, and although Genevieve did not wish to follow, she had no choice. Her father decided to enroll all his school-aged children within a year, and they would be among the first Aaniiih children to attend.

Eight-year-old Genevieve Healy may have felt as Gertrude Bonnin had after leaving her reservation at the same age to attend school: "frightened and bewildered as the captured young of a wild creature." Zitkála-Šá (Bonnin) wrote in naturalistic language (that likely reflected both a personal association with nature and a consciousness of her non-Native readership, which imagined Indians as primarily tied to nature) about the emotional scarring of her long-term separation from home: "Like a slender tree, I had been uprooted from my mother, nature, and God," she expressed. "I was shorn of my branches, which had waved in sympathy and love for home and friends. . . . Now a cold bare pole I seemed to be, planted in a strange earth." Genevieve Healy, a bare sapling, too, joined other Native American girls from reservations across Montana on a campus where the very ground on which they stood was steeped in a fresh history of land dispossession and martial intimidation. Like Carlisle Indian School in Pennsylvania, Fort Shaw's campus had recently been used as an active US military base. Some of Genevieve's classmates shared similar stories of winding up at this isolated school against their will and of being sent away by white fathers in the absence of, or against the protests of, Indigenous mothers.

Nearly a century earlier, Sacagawea had stepped into an equally uncertain future, stripped of family save for the two-month-old baby on her back. She was born into the Shoshone nation (or "Snake" tribe) of present-day Idaho and Montana. Her people lived in a vast and varied ecology stretching across the Rocky Mountains, inter-mountain prairies, and northwestern rivers. They moved seasonally across this terrain, spending time in summer and winter settle-ments and taking what they needed to sustain their homes (teepees made of hide), diets (hunting and gathering), and clothing (leather and fur) from bison herds. As a girl in the community of her birth, Sacagawea would have learned the mentally and physically demand-ing subsistence skills all women needed: identifying, collecting, and preparing wild plants; drying and preserving salmon; cooking bison meat and smaller game; cleaning and tanning buffalo hides; constructing and transporting teepees and other household implements; sewing and beading articles of clothing; and caring for children.

When she was an adolescent, Sacagawea's band departed from their seasonal settlement to travel eastward toward the headwaters of the Missouri River. The group set up a temporary camp in a seemingly peaceful spot where three streams fringed by cottonwood trees curved through the green and gold prairie grasses. But they were acting within a charged economic and political environment shaped by an increasing European presence, an international trade in bison hides, and frequent raiding. Suddenly, a Hidatsa raiding party attacked, scattering the Shoshone campers and taking three girls and four boys. Those girls—Sacagawea, Otter Woman, and Leaping Fish Woman—were transported over 500 miles eastward to the Knife River villages of the allied Hidatsa and Mandan nations. The three female captives were held in the lodge of Red Arrow, who intended to keep them as wives. One of them, Leaping Fish Woman, escaped and rejoined the Shoshones. Sacagawea and Otter Woman remained in this household for six months to two years.

In June of 1803, around the time of Sacagawea's captivity on the bluffs of the Missouri, Thomas Jefferson, the third president of the United States, spelled out detailed instructions to Meriwether Lewis (who would then recruit fellow Virginian William Clark), requesting observations "to be taken with great pains and accuracy" of the Indigenous people inhabiting the lands around the Missouri River. Jefferson wanted to know, among other things, "the names of the nations & their numbers; the extent and limits of their possessions; their relations with other tribes or nations; their language, traditions, monuments; their ordinary occupations . . . their food, clothing & domestic accommodations; the diseases prevalent among them, & the remedies they use; moral and physical circumstances which distinguish them from the tribes we know; peculiarities in their laws, customs & dispositions; and articles of commerce they may need to furnish." Jefferson did not want to instigate open conflict, neither did he plan, at that time, to expel Indigenous residents. Rather, he wanted intercourse with Native nations to follow a diplomatic course, so he further instructed Meriwether Lewis to treat Indigenous people in a "friendly & conciliatory manner" and to "satisfy them of it's [the expedition's] innocence."

But the mission was not innocent, in that it grew out of an existing policy of American national expansion into Indigenous lands and was intended "formally to extend American power up the Missouri and toward the mountains," writes one major historian of the expedition. Thomas Jefferson would soon augment his initial instructions in a letter, spelling out the kind of soft power he wanted Lewis to wield. Native people must be informed that the United States had "now become sovereigns of the country" and "without . . . diminution of the Indian rights of occupancy . . . are authorized to propose to them in direct terms the institution of commerce." In essence, Jefferson wanted Lewis and Clark to convey to representatives of Native nations that the United States had "become their fathers," the political sovereign with a higher authority to dictate commercial relations.

This was the diplomatic morass in which Sacagawea would become entangled in the spring of 1805. Historical sources differ on how Sacagawea, by then thirteen or fourteen, came into the hands of the trader Toussaint Charbonneau, a resident in one of the Hidatsa villages. Red Arrow may have lost Sacagawea and Otter

Woman to Charbonneau in an "all night gambling match," or he may have "sold" them to Charbonneau. At the time that she came into this forty-something Frenchman's household as his teenage "spouse," Sacagawea was not a free person. She had this unfree status in common with Harriet Tubman's mother, Rit, who was her temporal contemporary. So when Charbonneau offered his services as an interpreter to Lewis and Clark, he was also altering the course of Sacagawea's life. As the captains interviewed Charbonneau, they noticed his two Shoshone "wives," who had come from the lands the captains needed to cross. They hired Charbonneau, knowing they would need these women to translate when they entered Shoshone territory, and they solicited information from the young women, including requests for cartographic drawings.

In 1804, while Lewis, Clark, and their men wintered over in their fort near the Mandan villages, the approximately sixteen-year-old Sacagawea gave birth to her first child, whom Charbonneau named Jean-Baptiste. William Clark would later nickname the baby "Pomp," a reference to either Napoleon (the French commander) or Pompey (a Roman emperor)—a grandiose pet name like the hyperbolic and intentionally humorous classical names, such as Caesar and Hercules, that Southern slaveholders assigned to enslaved African Americans. By all indications, William Clark grew fond of Jean-Baptiste and likely used the nickname to express affection. At the same time, Clark was a Southerner from Virginia who grew up in a slaveholding family and had brought his own enslaved man since childhood, York, along on the expedition; he carried with him into the West the psychology of an enslaver for whom white superiority was assumed.

In April of 1805, after the snows had melted, Lewis and Clark's contingent was preparing to depart. Sacagawea would be compelled to accompany them and leave her pregnant friend Otter Woman, also around sixteen years old, behind. Sacagawea departed as the lone female in the company of over thirty men and one infant, whose life rested in her hands. During the journey that lasted more than a year, she had no privacy. She and the child slept with Charbonneau, Lewis, and Clark in a separate tent from the soldiers, who all camped in close quarters. Charbonneau may have been in the habit of physically abusing her, as Clark recorded in the expedition journals that he once criticized the Frenchman for "Strikeing his woman at their Dinner."

But it was Sacagawea, rather than Lewis, Clark, or Charbonneau, who had expertise in "the visible world of rivers, mountains, and plains" and the "sometimes invisible universe of Indian politics and European rivalries," as one historian of Native women's intercultural relations has put it. What the expedition needed, and what "Lewis and Clark took from Sacagawea," a historian of slavery notes, "was her knowledge." Early in the journey, near the Judith River in what is now central Montana, Sacagawea identified a pair of abandoned moccasins as bearing artistic markers of the Atsina nation, more commonly known today as Gros Ventres or Aaniiih people, Fort Shaw student Genevieve Healy's forebears.

As the expedition continued west across the northern plains and mountains, Sacagawea provided essential information that helped Lewis and Clark orient and interpret the geographical, political, and cultural zones around them. Many months later, on the return trip to St. Louis, she recognized landmarks in what is today the Bozeman Pass of the Rockies, advising Clark, who recorded: "The indian woman who has been of great Service to me as a pilot through this

Country recommends a gap in the mountain more South which I shall cross." Although she had a brief encounter with her brother, the Shoshone leader Cameahwait, and other members of her tribe near the three forks of the Missouri River (a reunion of great benefit to Lewis and Clark, who traded guns with Cameahwait for horses and guides), Sacagawea made most of this journey as an isolated young woman far from those who cared for her. Seeing Sacagawea afresh as a teenaged mother, as a shrewd interpreter of people, landscapes, and geopolitics, and as someone whose mental and physical prowess was exploited by others indicts the expedition she served and disrupts the popular notion of an Indian princess pantheon set against a romanticized natural backdrop.

Sacagawea's complex past was prologue to the next century. Like Sacagawea, the students at Fort Shaw experienced wrenching separations from their families, entered a foreign cultural environment that appropriated their work and skills, and drew on the outdoor upbringing of their childhoods to navigate the changed circumstances in which they found themselves. While bearing cumulative territorial, cultural, and psychological losses that Sacagawea could not have foreseen and insidious pressures of assimilation that she could not have imagined, these girls would maintain their Indigenous selfhood, and beyond that, use their boarding school educations to support their families and communities back home and push for political change at the national level.

Fort Shaw was built in a gorgeous place that cast deep shadows. Flowing near the Rocky Mountains in an area called the Sun Valley, the Sun River ripples even today with stunning reflective light. In the centuries before Euro-American arrival, this valley served as a hunting ground for Indigenous groups, including Blackfeet, Aaniiih–Gros Ventre, and Crow hunters. The land along the Sun River also provided a varied natural apothecary. The Blackfeet environmental historian Rosalyn LaPier writes that her grandfather's mother "used to travel one hundred miles south down to the Sun River near Fort Shaw to gather plants such as yucca, which they valued for its medicinal qualities." However, the influx of American settlers led to a shrinkage of Blackfeet hunting and gathering grounds, as was also the case for other tribal nations in the region. Blackfeet people mourned, in particular, the newcomers' rampant destruction of the cottonwood trees that graced the river and creek banks. While American settlers overharvested this wood to fuel steamboats along the Missouri, Blackfeet people prized it for the center pole in their major sacred ceremony.

In 1867, the US military raised a fort in the Sun Valley to defend white settlers who were traveling between the bustling fur trade town of Fort Benton (at the end point of steamboat routes on the Missouri River and the starting point of overland trails for travel and freight transport) and the city of Helena, by way of crossing at the Sun River. Four infantry companies set up a post along the river, purportedly "owing to the danger of the lives and properties of the white settlers." On July 4, 1867, officials renamed the military establishment Fort Shaw after the fallen Civil War commander Robert Gould Shaw, who had led the Black troops of the now-famous Massachusetts 54th regiment into heroic battle outside Charleston, South Carolina. And in this detail is another vexing facet of the Fort Shaw girls' basketball team story: this western fort bearing the name of a New Englander who fought for Black freedom had been built to curtail *Native* freedom. Soldiers at Fort Shaw were, as well, a biracial contingent. Most were white, but the final company to arrive was made up of African American infantrymen from Fort Assiniboine, situated to the northeast of the Sun River valley, roughly between Fort Benton and Fort Belknap. These soldiers from the 25th Infantry Black regiment stationed at Fort Shaw in 1890 to police Indigenous peoples would eventually fight in the Spanish American War and thereby advance American empire.

In 1891, the military shut down the fort, according to an internal Fort Shaw history, "after the Indians were subdued and restricted to reservations." Just one year later, in December 1892, the Office of Indian Affairs founded a school for the transformation of American Indian youth on those very grounds of contestation over Native mobility. Like the military forts that preceded some of them as a matter of design, boarding schools were, as major scholars of their history have put it, "sites of containment" applied to "a fundamentally political process." The outside grounds on which these schools stood contributed to that process and hence became politicized in the daily lives of students. At Fort Shaw, a history of power dynamics was already embedded in place before a single child arrived. Soldiers had sculpted the prairie into a virtual stage for postcolonial order, complete with imposed clearings, non-native plants, and the geometric configuration of built structures, broadcasting a message of control, organization, and change.

The children who encountered Fort Shaw at a mature enough age to interpret their surroundings must have been painfully aware that they were being housed, fed, and taught on a martial landscape. The configuration of the Fort Shaw Indian School slotted right into the preexisting exterior design, physical layout, and practical architecture of the former military post. The land had been culled into regimented order just months after the soldiers had pitched their tents. The soldiers had cleared the land to build the fort, culling cottonwood trees and taming prairie grasses. They then built a settlement in the shape of a square, locating communal buildings on one line of the square, placing a hospital, store, and chapel on the adjacent straight axis, locating officers' quarters opposite, and completing the form with a line of soldiers' barracks. The identical 400-square-foot dwelling houses made of "bullet proof" adobe bricks all faced the center of the square "in true fort style." To the north of the main square were the stables, barn, water pumping station, coal house, ice house, and the bank of the Sun River. The well-managed military site had "a caretaker [who] took care of the grounds and kept them in fine condition," and "grass, trees, and flowers . . . which made the fort a very attractive spot." Fort Shaw Indian School settled into these same grooves, repurposing the buildings as staff housing, classrooms, dormitories, and a dining hall; teaching industrial skills in outbuildings near the river; and incorporating the open land as sports and exhibition fields.

At military-inspired schools like Fort Shaw, discipline achieved by "military methods" was seen as necessary to force children into the strict cultural mold that educators intended for them. Children were made to dress alike, march in lines, adhere to dictated timetables, and comport themselves in an obedient, orderly manner. Matrons of the schools even kept strict watch on girls' reproductive cycles to monitor potential pregnancies, routinely inspecting menstrual rags for blood. A photograph of Fort Shaw students in 1910 captures the mood of this life of regimentation and confinement on their campus, picturing long rows of identically dressed boys in dark suits and girls in white dresses, flanked by formally appareled staff, rigidly posed in front of a line of stark buildings on the open plain.

At Fort Shaw School, like other schools in the government system, white administrators demeaned everything "Indian"—hygiene, dress, hair, speech, mannerisms, beliefs, and family ties. Children were taught to feel shame at the blankets they draped over their shoulders, the long and loose or braided hairstyles they wore, and the languages they spoke. When new students arrived at Fort Shaw and other schools of its kind, they were separated from siblings, inspected for lice, bathed, shorn of their hair, clothed in uniforms, made to march, discouraged from talking at mealtime, given new names, and prohibited from speaking their tribal languages anywhere on campus. Zitkála-Šá (Gertrude Bonnin) describes the hair-cutting initiation at her school as particularly traumatic. Her long hair was important to her sense of self, and she hated the rough, disrespectful handling by school officials that contrasted so starkly with how adults carefully touched her at home. When she realized what was about to befall her, little Gertrude ran and hid, then kicked and scratched before she was tied to a chair while her hair was forcibly shorn by a matron. Breaks from this harsh treatment and unfamiliar regimen were few and far between for boarding school children. Students at Fort Shaw would soon learn that the manual labor they performed as part of their industrial training would support the operations of the school—from the cooking, sewing, and laundry carried out by girls to the farming and livestock husbandry done by boys, who would produce much of the school's food supply. In keeping with the reformist view that tribal communities were detrimental to student advancement, Fort Shaw's superintendent tried to prevent pupils from returning home to their reservations during the summer.

Students, especially boys, routinely escaped from these schools. At Fort Shaw, runaways attempted to cover a hundred miles and more on foot to return to their home reservations. Fort Shaw officials dispatched staff members to track down absconding students and paid local settlers five dollars for the return of a child. When boarding school students ran away, they risked punishment and injury—and sometimes lost their lives. Still, this drastic course of action constituted a highly visible and especially disruptive resistance tactic. A group of Fort Shaw boys, like many boys at other schools, were jailed after leaving campus without permission after dark. The school superintendent locked some of the kids into the fort's guardhouse when they returned of their own accord from playing along the riverbank. But the boys who were not yet confined aided the others, breaking into the manual training room and collecting tools, which they used to break into the guardhouse, nearly destroying it, to free their trapped friends. Failure to act in accordance with school rules resulted in sound punishment, from the draconian corrections of jailing and physical abuse to the taxing consequences of extra cleaning duties.

The rebellion of Native youth against the cultural and physical confinement of boarding schools could take many forms—from escaping, to setting fires, to sabotaging school supplies, to subtly breaking institutional rules, to secretly retaining cultural practices. Looking at Fort Shaw's female basketball team from the perspective of freedoms that could be claimed outside enhances this catalog. A game billed as thoroughly modern, basketball could be played indoors or outdoors, by boys or girls. It developed in the East and traveled westward as the first major sport invented in the United States. And the Fort Shaw girls would propel themselves to the center of this story when they played the first basketball game in Montana on an outdoor field at their school and later participated in the first national demonstration of the sport, again outdoors, at the St. Louis World's Fair.

The Fort Shaw players may have been resisting the strictures of their educational institution when they embraced this new sport and successfully lobbied school administrators to back their activities. In a learning environment that insisted on the suppression of inner desires and the control of bodily movement, especially for girls, the players pressed for something *they* wanted: to play this physically exerting, competitive game. Administrators at Fort Shaw made room for basketball as part of a new physical education program and then promoted the sport when they realized a standout team could bring glory to the school. By all indications, the basketball craze at Fort Shaw—and across the state of Montana—originated with Native teens and girls. The Fort Shaw players lived and learned on colonized grounds, but they also took advantage of the movement afforded by their chosen sport to bend the cage of their campus. Through determination, athleticism, and team building across tribal lines, these girls forged an unexpected escape from spatial and cultural confinement, demonstrating along the way that Native girls could compete on the white world's uneven playing field.

As the team's biographers Linda Peavy and Ursula Smith recount, a young woman who stood out at first mainly for her academics most likely launched Fort Shaw's basketball history. In 1893, when enrollments ticked upward at Fort Shaw, Superintendent William Winslow identified young boarding school graduates to bring on board as assistants. One of these junior staff members was a seventeen-year-old Blackfeet girl named Josephine (Josie) Langley, who had been "born in the shadow of Old Fort Shaw." The child of a Blackfeet mother and a white former military scout, Josephine was at first enrolled at St. Peter's Mission School, a Catholic institution near the Sun River, from the age of nine. St. Peter's also happens to have been the workplace of Mary Fields, one of the best-known African American historical figures in early Montana.

Like Harriet Tubman, Mary Fields had been born into Southern slavery. Following her emancipation, she moved from West Virginia to Ohio with her former enslavers and then followed their daughter to a convent. Fields worked as a domestic at the convent, occupying her own room and receiving pay. She remained with these Ursuline nuns for years, traveling with them by choice from Toledo, Ohio, to eastern and then central Montana. Between 1885 and 1895, she lived and worked at St. Peter's Mission outside the town of Cascade, raising a large vegetable garden, keeping hundreds of chickens, and hunting to keep the school supplied with food. Quite suddenly, when Fields was in her sixties, she was expelled from her home and workplace. Against the wishes of the nuns, and Mary Fields herself, the Great Falls bishop with authority over the mission enterprise charged Fields with inappropriate language and behavior and insisted that she leave St. Peter's. With the nuns' assistance, Fields attained a federal mail carrier position to transport parcels between Great Falls and St. Peter's. From 1895 to 1903, she carried packages, and sometimes travelers, in her horse-drawn coach through both fair and foul weather. She became legendary in Montana history as a physically robust, gun-toting, pants-wearing "female wagon master who freighted mail"—a stereotypically masculinized, racialized image. Mary Fields, who often wore skirts and a man's coat to stay warm in the harsh winter weather, would have worked at St. Peter's during Josephine Langley's student years in the mid-1880s; she was also said to love the sport of baseball so much that she attended men's games regularly later in life. Whether Mary Field's enjoyment of sports had any impact on a young Josephine Langley is a matter of intriguing speculation.

Josephine excelled at St. Peter's Mission School, garnering staff support and applying to Carlisle to train as a teacher. She was rejected from Carlisle, however, because she had trachoma, a chronic and often painful eye infection that could cause blindness. Trachoma was especially prevalent in boarding schools, which struggled with the spread of other dangerous contagious diseases as well, such as influenza and tuberculosis. After receiving the disappointing news from Carlisle, Josephine Langley accepted an assistant position at Fort Shaw, where she again shined. Josephine's performance in her first year on staff at Fort Shaw gained her the notice of Richard Henry Pratt, superintendent of Carlisle, who was visiting Fort Shaw on a recruiting trip. Pratt invited Langley to return to Pennsylvania with him as a student. In 1895, she traveled to Carlisle to formally train as a teacher.

At Carlisle, which was older and larger than Fort Shaw, Josephine Langley first observed girls playing a sport called "basket ball." As an enrolled student, the nineteen-year-old learned how to play the game, which had only recently been invented and then introduced to female students in nearby New England. Developed by James Naismith at Springfield College in Massachusetts in 1891, basketball was generally played according to rules meant for boys, which allowed for faster-paced, rougher action across a full indoor or outdoor court. In 1894, Senda Berenson, a physical education teacher at Smith College in Northampton, Massachusetts, began to adapt the game's rules to make it acceptable for women. The first recorded game of women's basketball occurred indoors at Smith, where young women competed before a cheering same-sex crowd and played according to an early version of what would later be codified as "girls' rules." From New England, the game traveled to Carlisle Indian School, perhaps by way of representatives of the YMCA. At Carlisle, Josephine Langley became a skilled player. When she was forced to abandon her studies nine months early due to the resurgence of her eye infection, Langley returned to Montana. She rejoined the Fort Shaw staff, bringing back a game that would change girls' lives.

Upon her return to Fort Shaw, Josephine Langley achieved a promotion, accepting the post of physical culture instructor for girls in January of 1896, a time when physical education was not yet fully incorporated into most boarding school curricula. She may have integrated basketball drills into her first physical education classes, and she also encouraged participation in the sport outside of class. As a teacher, she mentored and trained a cadre of girls who missed their families and reservation communities and, like Genevieve Healy, may have pined for former childhood afternoons spent running and riding outside. Josephine introduced basketball as an extracurricular to those girls who showed an interest, borrowing a soccer ball from the boys' athletic program when Superintendent Winslow claimed a lack of funds to purchase a ball and baskets for the girls. Josephine Langley and her first recruits made do with the supplies they had and pressed on with their training.

The students who followed Josephine's lead may have embraced the new game as a distraction from feelings of homesickness. Perhaps they enjoyed a physical outlet that allowed them to recapture the freedom of movement that they had loved as girls at home. Or maybe they welcomed the sense of collectivity that came from playing together in an institutional context that emphasized individuality. Some of the girls who would join the Fort Shaw basketball team had not only run, jumped, and ridden horses back home, but had also likely played or watched competitive Indigenous ball games in which women participated, such as "double ball" (Shoshone, Bannock, and Dakota), "shinny" (Shoshone, Crow, Ute, and Sioux), and "kicking the ball" (Crow). While basketball was a novelty to these girls and to everyone else in the United States, exerting themselves physically for the joy of it, using balls in competitive play, and acting as cooperative members of a team was not. In the years to come, when the Fort Shaw players would astonish hundreds, then thousands, of spectators by crushing every other team they met on the field, they left sports commentators shaking their heads at the marvelous display of speed—and teamwork. It is quite possible that the very tribalism and collectivism that the boarding school attempted to drain from students were among the hidden strengths that turned Fort Shaw's team into champions.

Throughout the fall of 1896, Josephine Langley taught her students how to handle a basketball on the grassy field outside the classrooms. She designated an area near the parade grounds where students performed at the end of each school year and managed to have baskets hung. She drilled the girls for hours outside of required physical education class time, teaching them how to dribble, pass, and shoot. Among the first students to train with Josephine Langley were Genevieve Healy and Katie Snell, from Fort Belknap; sisters Lizzie Wirth and Nettie Wirth and Mattie Hayes, from the Fort

Peck Reservation; and Belle Johnson, from the Blackfeet Reservation. They may have felt a sense of relief in exerting themselves at
challenging tasks other than domestic manual labor, which took up
much of their daily schedule, and the routinized physical education
exercises required of their curriculum.

When the chill and snows of winter settled over Fort Shaw, Josephine Langley moved training to an indoor court, repurposing the
military dance hall on campus. That spring, she divided her players
into two squads of five students each. At the end-of-year ceremo-
nies, the squads competed on their outside field before an audience of
school staff, parents, and visitors. Playing by the fast-paced boys' rules
taught by their coach, the Fort Shaw girls bolted across the prairie
grasses, dribbling, throwing, and shooting at a dizzying speed, and
nearly tying each other in a nail-biting final score of 7 to 6. It was a
rare thing for non-Native people to see girls of any race use their bodies with such controlled strength in competitive sport. It was likewise
rare for Native parents to see their children accorded regard by white
onlookers and for Fort Shaw administrators to glimpse the potential their students held to captivate an audience. This match on Fort
Shaw's grounds in the spring of 1897 would turn out to be the first
basketball game witnessed in the state of Montana. For the impres-
sionable young girls on the field that day—experiencing the rush of
somatic exhilaration and the power of movement that still belonged to
them even in this constricting place—we can imagine that this game
was a moment of awakening. Perhaps the Fort Shaw girls learned on
that prairie playing field a key lesson of the successful boarding school
runaway: that movement was a form of freedom. Perhaps the girls also
noticed that they could be free in this small way within full view of
Fort Shaw authorities, who approved of adding girls' basketball to the

athletic program and would soon use Josephine Langley's initiative and her students' skills to promote the school.

Josephine Langley's inaugural effort at Fort Shaw echoed the development of popular athletics programs at other boarding schools. "The Indian boarding school system had become a hotbed of athletic talent," writes a leading scholar of Native American cultural history, who notes that the male students channeled this talent toward mixed outcomes, in which competitive sports "could be seen as part of a refigured warrior tradition" but also "provided entrée into American society—a chance to beat whites at their own games." If male football players were tapping into an Indigenous warrior tradition even while playing an American sport that could yield assimilative access, female basketball players were drawing on a tradition of women's outdoor physicality while playing a sport that also demonstrated their "Americanness." Being a boarding school athlete, like being a boarding school student, was a double-edged experience of accommodation and resistance. But along that knife's edge, the girls of Fort Shaw's team could recapture some of the outdoor freedom that young Native girls had enjoyed, as well as community regard for somatic mastery that Native women had earned over generations before them.

For Gertrude Bonnin, writing as Zitkála-Šá, this was a tradition of "wild freedom" associated with being "as free as the wind that blew my hair, and no less spirited than a bounding deer." For Aaniiih student Genevieve Healy, this was the tradition, in paraphrase, of being a "wild child" and "riding across the open range." As northern plains girls matured into women prior to American colonization, this "wild" sensibility included outdoor exploits requiring skill, strength, and bravery—from gathering plants and culling rice, to gathering water and moving camp, to accompanying male hunting parties, and, on rare occasions, going to war. It also included a core component of sensory-somatic "vitality"—the liberated feeling of moving one's body in a fully sensed and conceptualized environment. As the Dakota educator and anthropologist Ella Deloria wrote in a 1924 report on Indian girls' health at boarding schools, the Native American "great-grandmother seemed to have unusual vitality and endurance. It could not have been otherwise under her conditions of life, for she had continuous exercise from her childhood to her grave." In contrast, Deloria noted, the "Indian girl of today" lived a house-bound and school-bound lifestyle requiring restrictive clothing and military regimentation and lacking in training "for anything in particular which involves rigorous muscular activity." Far from encouraging girls to flex their muscles, boarding school educators tried to compel bodily restriction and control, seeking "to sever the intimacy and sensory connections the children had developed with their homelands," as a scholar of Native family history has put it.

In creative opposition to this control, two prominent boarding school graduates, both writers, intentionally adopted the rhetoric of wildness. In using the language of wildness in her memoir, Zitkála-Šá reclaimed the word "wild" and its meanings from the critical voices of white school administrators who used it as a pejorative. Josephine Waggoner, a Lakota student at Hampton Institute in Virginia who later compiled hundreds of pages of tribal oral history, also chose the language of wildness to describe an embrace of home and motion. In evocative phrasing found in one of her notebooks, Waggoner captured this sense of bold, kinesthetic movement that could belong to girls and women outside. She wrote in 1934, "When the hills and the open ranges are calling, jolt your ribs in a wild ride over the plains" and then referred to a "sage brush philosophy that caress the trails." Her meaning is perhaps elusive, especially when rendered in English, but we can gather from her words an implication of philosophical and physical orientation—a way of thinking, moving, and being—that arises from intimacy with the natural, outdoor world.

There is no Lakota word for "nature" because nature is "just what *is*," says Emily Levine, an ecologist who worked closely with Waggoner's descendants while editing Waggoner's papers for publication. Josephine Waggoner was, in Levine's words, a "prairie girl" who tenderly described South Dakota geography and wrote about the coldness of the western mountains and the strangeness of the New England hills. This was a different valence of prairie than the one conveyed by Laura Ingalls Wilder's popular *Little House on the Prairie* series (1932–1943), in which the idealized white American family "domesticates" and "civilizes" formerly Indigenous land and then views "Indians" as intruders. Waggoner embraced an open-armed, relational conception of her prairie home and carried that view of place wherever she went. As Levine put it: "Everywhere she lived—at Apple Creek, near Fort Yates, her stay in the Powder River country, her allotment on Hay Creek at the western edge of the reservation—Josephine was intimately connected to the land." Josephine Waggoner's notion of a sagebrush philosophy gestures toward this sense of physical, spiritual, and cultural connection to one's outdoor home. And this holistic physicality was also intellectual. In her explanation of "Land as Pedagogy," the contemporary Nishnaabeg scholar Leanne Betasamosake Simpson offers language that opens up Waggoner's words. "Coming to know is the pursuit of whole-body intelligence practiced in the context of freedom," Simpson writes; Indigenous learning comes "both *from* the land and *with* the land."

Boarding school educators seemed to want to strip all this wisdom and wonder away. They attempted to button Indigenous girls up into proper Victorian dresses, to hem these girls into tidy kitchens and parlors, to pin them down to a somatically constrained gender culture, to steal their birthright of exuberant movement on their own lands. They sought to allow only those "remnant" behaviors of traditional "Indian-ness" that fell into what Native education theorists Tsianina Lomawaima and Teresa McCarty have described as "safety zones." But former students like Bonnin and Waggoner resisted through a rhetoric of wildness, and girls like the Fort Shaw players resisted through an embrace of sport. Enacting "wild" outdoor motion may have been one way that boarding school girls like them "incorporate[ed] forbidden Indian culture into their daily lives."

Ella Deloria contended in her report that the introduction of "good rousing games" in school could help restore the "Indian girl of today's" overall health and "mental and spiritual" well-being. Even before Deloria made this assessment, basketball had emerged as a favorite team sport for boarding school girls. Girls at Haskell Indian School in Lawrence, Kansas, like girls at Carlisle and Fort Shaw, played the sport with apparent zeal. At Haskell, where Deloria taught physical education and gathered material for her study in the 1920s, the girls played basketball using boys' rules (as opposed to the normative girls' rules) and formed a competitive team as early as 1900. The sport was so popular at Haskell that girls played informally with wastebaskets in their dorms, risking correction by school staff, who proved surprisingly lenient. The Haskell girls' basketball team traveled across Kansas, playing competitive games against other schools. When Indigenous girls played sports at American boarding schools, they struck a delicate balance between exhibiting white Victorian femininity, as they were instructed to do in these institutions, and enacting the Indigenous femininities of their home communities, which included a holistic physicality outdoors.

The Fort Shaw girls' basketball team grew and matured over a decade, even as Fort Shaw's student body expanded to include students from Idaho and Wyoming. Métis student Emma Rose Sansaver, who had been raised in a mixed-race Indigenous settlement between Fort Assiniboine and the city of Havre and had attended St. Paul's School on the Fort Belknap Reservation, enrolled at Fort Shaw and joined the team, as did Genie Butch Rose, from Fort Peck, and the Lemhi Shoshone student, Minnie Burton, from the Lemhi Reservation in Idaho, who would later be showered with the rousing cheer "Shoot, Minnie, Shoot!" Meanwhile, other female teams were forming across the state. In 1898, a white women's team known as the Farmerettes formed at the Montana Agricultural College in Bozeman (now Montana State University), and women's teams began springing up in the mining city of Butte and the university town of Missoula. As illness benched Josephine Langley, who had previously played on the field with her team, a white assistant on staff originally from the Northeast, Sadie Malley, continued to train the Fort Shaw girls according to the boys' rules, which eastern women's sports programs typically avoided.

In February of 1901, Genevieve Healy pressed Sadie Malley about the future of the team, asking when they would have uniforms and competitive matches. In 1902, the year that the *Great Falls Daily Leader* newspaper announced "Basketball is the Thing," the new superintendent of Fort Shaw, F. C. Campbell, arranged for a series of games across Montana. Superintendent Campbell also assumed for himself the formal title of coach, overshadowing the essential

The collegiate women's basketball team vigorously plays on a field in Missoula, Montana, circa 1900. Jeannette Rankin, the first woman elected to the US Congress in 1916, is one of the pictured players. Used by permission of the Montana Historical Society.

and foundational contribution of women coaches and trainers. The Fort Shaw basketball team set off on tour in the spring of 1903, playing their "most brilliant game," according to the *Great Falls Leader*, against the Farmerettes before a crowd of eight hundred people. Hailed as "the first shutout in Montana basketball history," this game, a rematch with the previously defeated Farmerettes (36 to 9), favored the Fort Shaw high school students over the Bozeman college students for the win of 20 to 0. The Fort Shaw team played and won several games in a "loosely cobbled girls basketball league," defeating teams from Butte, Boulder, Bozeman, Missoula, and the Sun River valley, and becoming Montana state champions in 1903. That summer, they played a series of exhibition games across a line of towns toward the northern band of the state: Fort Benton, Havre, Chinook, Harlem, Glasgow, and Poplar. The team traveled by train, expanding their geographical and social horizons and leaving behind the spatial confines and strict rules of campus. Two locations were close to their family homes and may have been attended by relatives.

Harlem bordered the Fort Belknap Reservation, and Poplar was on the Fort Peck Reservation. For these demonstration matches, the team divided into squads as Josephine Langley had trained them to do years before. Now there were stripes on the girls' dickies and the large embroidered letters F and S (for Fort Shaw) on the white collars of their elaborate uniforms, which also bore the color of their squad—blue or red (or "brown" in some press coverage at the time).

Playing basketball brought girls at Fort Shaw an astonishing degree of mobility for their place, time, race, gender, and age. For their matches, the girls donned navy worsted wool bloomer uniforms

Fort Shaw basketball team members sit on a field with spectators in the background during the St. Louis World's Fair. Note the carefully sewn white letters and stripes that add detail to their uniforms. Front row: G. Butch, B. Johnson, E. Sansaver; Back row: N. Wirth, Mr. McCutcheon, K. Snell, M. Burton. Courtesy of the Missouri Historical Society.

(closed-legged and gathered at the hems) that they had sewn for themselves and surely preferred over the heavy, awkward skirts that typified the boarding school uniform, even though these bloomers were still more physically restrictive than the soft, loose dresses and leggings that many Native girls wore at home. At the same time that travel allowed Fort Shaw players more freedom, it also exposed them to racial prejudice rooted in the perception of American Indian backwardness. White onlookers flocked to these games by the dozens and hundreds, in part to view the novel sport and in part to watch Indians play it. Because Superintendent Campbell expected his team to put on pregame theatrical and musical shows, the players were on view for white crowds who paid fifty cents per person for a ticket. Performances featured the athletes themselves in dramatic scenes from classical literature, as well as an entourage of other talented students from the school—the band, the mandolin club (which included some basketball players), and a Vaudeville-esque child comic.

In artistic segments of graceful pantomime and poetry recitation from Henry Wadsworth Longfellow's *Song of Hiawatha*, the basketball players of Fort Shaw dressed in long white gowns with their hair artfully swept up and beribboned, or they wore their traditional Indigenous regalia and styled their hair in braids. Longfellow's popular poem, published in 1855 and based on the ethnographic writing of Jane Johnston Schoolcraft's husband, was a telling choice for reenactment, as the verse presented a savage yet romanticized Indian warrior of the past whose story unfolds against the backdrop of a setting sun. These poetic vignettes were not only meant to captivate audiences. They were also crafted to demonstrate the school's success in civilizing students by exhibiting Native traditional styles and

The Fort Shaw basketball team poses for a photograph in the traditional dresses they often wore during dramatic performances, 1906–1907. Used by permission of the Montana Historical Society.

mythic deeds as quaintly archaic and by illustrating the students' cultural distance from these former aesthetics and practices. Thus, as the team traveled and played basketball, they also performed their own assimilation before white crowds. In a disturbing point of intersection with African American history of the kind we saw in the naming of Fort Shaw after a Civil War hero, some of these skits involved Native students wearing blackface makeup and acting out scenes that caricatured African Americans—common fare of popular American minstrel shows meant to entertain white audiences. Publicly disparaging Black people was, by the late 1800s and early 1900s, a national pastime. Ironically, when Fort Shaw staff encouraged students to darken their already brown faces like white actors did, they silently signaled the students' progress toward acculturation and "civilization" by emphasizing the students' distance from and rejection of blackness.

These student performances conveyed racial and cultural subtexts that juxtaposed white and Indian ways, leaving viewers with their sense of white superiority and modernity confirmed. The Montana print press contributed to this comparison, racializing the athletic contests even further with headlines like "White Girls against Reds" and a description of the girls as "full-blooded Indians" and "half-breeds." In at least one cartoon, a newspaper portrayed the Fort Shaw players stereotypically as disheveled and unfeminine. These racially tinged depictions and comments stung, reminding the players of how their people were denigrated in broader society. Genevieve Healy is quoted by the team's biographers as having said resentfully, "They're going to see how half-breeds play basketball."

Without question, the Fort Shaw girls did demonstrate their superiority in the sport. They were, at the same time, still students in a government boarding school that imposed physical and psychological hardships on them, their peers, and their families. While the girls were traveling across the state, having purchased a degree of freedom from their school's strict regime by way of sport, students back on campus continued to run away and suffer punishment. In the winter of 1904, two seven-year-old boys absconded, attempting to get back home to Fort Belknap. The boys were George Snell and Fred Kuhnahan, the younger brother and cousin of team member Katie Snell. Fred died of exposure. George survived after having been "badly frozen." Katie, who had been on tour in a hotel at the time of the incident, was reportedly devastated at this loss.

In this moment of relative license to travel the state as athletes, set against the strictures of Fort Shaw's campus, the girls' team received an invitation to participate in the 1904 St. Louis World's Fair. Organizers planned this fair, formally called the Louisiana Purchase Exposition, to advertise the thriving midwestern host city of St. Louis and to celebrate American accomplishment upon the centennial anniversary of Meriwether Lewis and William Clark's expedition to the West. "Massive in scope" and "utopian in intent," it was the largest world's fair to date at that time anywhere in the world, featuring 128 acres of pavilions on over 1,240 acres of land in Forest Park and presenting to the public novel culinary delights like the ice cream cone, cotton candy, and hamburger. The event would showcase American progress and validate the country's imperial reach, which by then extended across and beyond the continent, through Native nations within the borders of the United States as well as vast swaths of the Southwest and Pacific Coast (following the war with Mexico in 1846) and the Pacific and Caribbean islands of Hawaii, Puerto Rico, and the Philippines (following the Hawaiian annexation and the 1898 Spanish-American War). The fairgrounds would include public art and monuments, including a life-sized stone statue of Sacagawea, commissioned of the New York sculptor Bruno Zimm, which was positioned on the eastern edge of the park on a major esplanade.

To highlight what St. Louis organizers and promoters viewed as American modernity and superiority, the fair would also exhibit live Indigenous peoples of color from around the globe, taking to new extremes efforts to elevate America before the eyes of the world through the mechanism of race. World's fairs, as one ethnic studies scholar writes, "were stages upon which ideas of empire and progress were publicly displayed. But at the Louisiana Purchase Exposition in

St. Louis, exhibitions of non-Western people and cultures reached a pinnacle. Indeed, organizers constructed exhibits to educate the public about racial progress and hierarchy." Key to the display of these "foreigners" and to the larger message of American greatness was racial difference. "America" was coded as white, as was the country's cultural and technological advancement. And the "primitive" people placed on display for St. Louis fairgoers were offered as America's "foil[s]"—uncivilized individuals from uncivilized cultures who existed on a lower level of the racial ladder.

Native Americans within the United States had a role to play in this visual drama, too—as evidence not only of the innate inferiority of racialized Indigenous peoples, but also, in the case of boarding school students, the possibilities for transformation and elevation as promised by US acculturation policies. "Many of the fair's Indian exhibits were 'living ones,'" writes one leading boarding school historian, "designed to both portray Indians in a variety of primitive contexts but also the race's evolutionary progress, the schoolhouse being a prime source of this progress." Within the fair's excessive setting of fantasy and invention, a manufactured "Indian Reservation" housed Indigenous people from the United States (mainly from nations within the original Louisiana Purchase boundaries) and abroad (from Argentina, the Philippines, Japan, and central Africa). Nearly three thousand Indigenous people were invited to participate in the fair by living on the grounds and performing their "traditional" ways for visitor observation. A subset of these performers would be children and teens from America's federal Indian schools.

When fair organizers contacted Fort Shaw's superintendent, they sought more than a basketball demonstration for their guests. They wanted Fort Shaw's star athletes to join 140 other boarding school students at the Indian Exhibit, where fair planners had a Model Indian School constructed atop a slope called Indian Hill. The Model Indian School with its "transformed boys and girls," as fair organizers described them, was an island apart from the "Reservation" and purposefully situated on "the highest ground in Forest Park." Just as the establishment of boarding schools on former military posts used landscape to send a message about the expectation of order and submission, the Model Indian School's location on a hill was a "visual symbol of the federal government's achievements in directed acculturation."

There, real students from existing boarding schools would live and study during the fair, with their activities visible to attendees. Ten Fort Shaw girls, described by Superintendent Campbell in a school press release as "quiet little ladies," would carry out the daily work of a typical boarding school day, perform the dramatic shows polished on the road in Montana, and of course, play ball. To prepare for this once in a lifetime opportunity, after a series of indoor matches across the state in 1903, the girls practiced on the old field that Josephine Langley (who had recently married a fellow staff member in the Fort Shaw Chapel) had originally prepared for them.

In June of 1904, the Fort Shaw girls rode the train to St. Louis, preparing to take up residence at the Model Indian School on grounds just as politicized as those they had left. In the impressive classical building that was a "functional stage set," they joined other selected students from Chilocco, Haskell, Genoa, and Sacaton Indian schools in a regimented daily schedule that would have been familiar to them all, except their activities were now on display for public viewing. On the day the Indian Model School and adjacent Anthropology Building opened, ten thousand fairgoers visited. The

Model Indian School became a popular exhibit at the fair, and the
Fort Shaw girls' dramatic and musical performances were among the
top attractions.

The Fort Shaw players kept an exacting schedule, studying and
carrying out domestic duties during the school day, performing dra-
mas and concerts in the late afternoons on an alternating schedule,
and playing two exhibition basketball games per week against each
other and other players in residence at the Model Indian School.
The Fort Shaw girls won every Model Indian School game, including against male opponents. They soon faced challenges from local
high schools and summarily beat a team from nearby Illinois as well
as St. Louis Central High's team, the Missouri state champions,
just before the fourth of July. Press accounts raved about the speed,
finesse, and teamwork of the Fort Shaw players. But not all spectators
were pleased—it must have been difficult for some midwesterners to
watch American Indian girls repeatedly best white American girls.
Perhaps this is why a local basketball coach scouted the Fort Shaw
games, charted the team's strengths and weaknesses, and selected
star alumnae from past Missouri state championship teams to challenge Fort Shaw in the fall.

In early August, on what were termed "Anthropology Days,"
the Fort Shaw team and other Indigenous athletes played in a set of
events alternately labeled the "Aboriginal Games" and the "Special
Olympics." Organized by the athletic director of the fair and by the
head anthropologist who had been hired to educate the public about
white American and northern European superiority over other races
and nations, these games were set up to pit savagery against civilization. Indigenous athletes from around the world would face one
another in a test of their athletic ability. Their performance would

then be compared with that of "civilized" athletes who were playing in the regular Olympic Games occurring during the fair.

As part of the "Special Olympics," the Fort Shaw girls were scheduled to scrimmage before spectators in a high-profile exhibition game at Francis Field. There they would be scrutinized in accordance with contradictory but equally racist expectations, contending that Indigenous people were naturally more athletic than whites and hence would do well in the games, *or* that Indigenous people were less physically vigorous than whites and would therefore do worse. The Fort Shaw team divided into two squads, the Reds and the Blues, and played against each other, their only true competition. Days later, all the Fort Shaw girls were awarded a single silver trophy engraved with the words: "World's Fair St. Louis, 1904 Basket Ball Won by Fort Shaw Team." The Model Indian School superintendent put the trophy, along with the students, on display in the building. In September, the Fort Shaw girls met the all-white, handpicked St. Louis All-Stars (also called the Missouri All-Stars) at Kulage Park in what was expected to be a formidable contest. In a two-out-of-three games playoff series, the Fort Shaw girls dealt the All-Stars crushing blows and earned widespread recognition as "champions of the world."

There was genuine triumph in this cumulative victory. As a Native American team—made up of girls, no less—who had bested American teams in an entirely modern sport, the Fort Shaw players challenged assumptions about Indian backwardness *and* women's physical weakness, breaking with mainstream cultural norms about what Native people *and* women could do, how they could do it, and where. Even so, hypotheses about Indigenous physical and mental fitness as compared to that of whites were tested on the fairgrounds, including at the Model Indian School. There, in the cooler autumn months, Fort Shaw players and other Native students were subjected to pseudoscientific racial study, including cranial measurements, so that test results could be compared with those of other fair participants and attendees.

The Fort Shaw players left St. Louis with enhanced fame. But they had also been exploited, displayed by adults expecting to demonstrate Indigenous people's inferiority, a notion that had undergirded and rationalized the advance of US colonialism into their western nations. Yet even as the Fort Shaw players had been subjected to this mistreatment, they may have gained broader knowledge and inner strength from meeting other Indigenous people from around the country and around the world, developing an "ever emerging and expanding Indigenous consciousness" and turning the St. Louis World's Fair into one among many "moments of colonial celebrations of empire [that] may have inadvertently served anticolonial purposes."

Genevieve Healy wanted to remember her weeks at the World's Fair. She inscribed in the memory book of teammate Emma Sansaver: "Darling Emma . . . All I ask of you is to remember N. J. and I as long as can. Don't forget the good times we have spent in St. Louie. Your Friend [for]ever." These sentiments suggested that theirs was a collective, rather than individual, experience of triumph. After graduation from Fort Shaw, many of the championship team members returned to their home reservations to support and raise families, living out an attachment to community life that formal education could not extinguish. Several of the women became employees at government boarding schools. This number of school staff members included Josephine Langley, the team's original coach, who served as a matron at the Cut Bank Indian boarding school

Fort Shaw team players huddle at halftime in front of the Model Indian School on the St. Louis World's Fair grounds, October 8, 1904. The photograph, passed down in the family of Emma Rose Sansaver, is shown here by generous permission of Barbara and Gina Winters, with additional thanks to Linda Peavy.

near her home reservation, Blackfeet, in Montana. Minnie Burton, whose accurate throws had once given rise to raucous cheers, later worked as a seamstress in the Indian School Service at her home reservation, Lemhi Shoshone, in Idaho. Nettie Wirth, of Fort Peck, joined the staff of the team's alma mater as an assistant seamstress. Katie Snell returned to the Fort Belknap Reservation, raised a family, and, according to interviews with her daughter and grandchildren, told stories about Fort Shaw and St. Louis on winter nights. Genevieve Healy remained at Fort Shaw until she was twenty. In 1908, she returned to Fort Belknap, too, where she had seven children, sang while she worked, and regaled her family with tales about playing basketball in St. Louis. The last team member to pass away in 1981 at the age of ninety-three, Healy had granddaughters, great-granddaughters, and great-nieces who all played on their high school basketball teams. It is left to our historical imagination to wonder how these former athletes may have passed on an Indigenous tradition of women's physical vitality as administrators, staff members, mothers, and grandmothers—but imagine, we should.

Fort Shaw Indian School closed its doors in the spring of 1910. A school history attributes a downturn in enrollment to the construction of other boarding schools and laments the decline of the old military grounds, where "the lawns were neglected and the houses were no longer kept in repair." Within twenty years, the government boarding school system would come under scrutiny after a 1928 report written by the scholar Lewis Meriam and commissioned by the Department of the Interior exposed the unethical recruitment practices, harsh disciplinary methods, inadequate dietary provisions, high degree of disease, and poor educational outcomes across the system.

The first decades of the new century would be hard on these women who had once been Fort Shaw boarding school girls. Their people and lands remained under relentless assault as the reservation era transformed into the allotment era, in which the federal government targeted communal tribal lands for subdivision and redistribution. They struggled to maintain family ranches and often worked at low-paying jobs. In a moment that is as heartbreaking as it is unjust, Minnie Burton would give birth to a daughter on the trail while her people were being forcibly marched to a new reservation (Fort Hall, Idaho) in 1907. Despite loss and heartache, these women who had once been girls outdoors applied the lessons of their school days, pushing beyond the boundaries of their proscribed places in a colonized landscape and winning the game that was survival.

BLUE MOONS

———

Remember why Harriet Tubman went south. She didn't
have to. . . . But if she wanted to tell an everlasting truth
about freedom that would ring across the planet, a
message for the ages, she had to live free in
unfree space. It was the only way to
bring us all with her.

—Alexis Pauline Gumbs, *Undrowned: Black Feminist Lessons
from Marine Mammals*, 2020

It took a plague to make some people realize
that things *could* change.

—Lauren Oya Olamina in Octavia E. Butler,
Parable of the Sower, 1993

OUR HIKE THROUGH the Dakota plains, Montana mountains,
Maryland woods, Massachusetts meadows, and St. Louis
streets have led us here—to a sense of how outdoor spaces have been
sites of girlhood learning and sometimes even training grounds for
later feats. From Sacagawea to Louisa May Alcott, from Harriet
Tubman to Zitkála-Šá, American girls of many backgrounds in

the nineteenth century and early twentieth century expanded their minds, honed their characters, and developed their skills outside. Their varied conceptualizations of inside versus outside, nature versus culture, and margin versus center shaped their intellectual, physical, and emotional interactions with complex social spheres and ultimately led to cultural and political change that expanded freedom, visibility, respect, and rights.

How might girls and young women constructively apply outdoor experience today when the world outside is still alluring, still instructive, still treacherous, but also altered by a new set of social, political, and ecological conditions? We can look to more recent historical examples as guides. In the late twentieth century, notable trailblazing women have sometimes been former girls outdoors, with trenchant messages for our times.

The Chinese American activist Grace Lee Boggs was once a girl whose renegade spirit found room to grow outdoors. Over much of the twentieth century and part of the twenty-first, Grace Lee Boggs was a thought leader for the city of Detroit. After earning her PhD in philosophy, Grace Lee married the African American labor rights activist James Boggs and became an outspoken advocate of urban farming, cooperative community, and political renewal. For Grace Lee Boggs, regeneration of the city began with the soil. She spent the last decades of her centenarian life reimagining how residents could live and work together on well-tended urban grounds and sharing her social criticisms and proposed solutions through writing and speeches.

Grace was born in Providence, Rhode Island, in 1915, the daughter of Chinese immigrants, and she spent many of her growing up years in New York City. Her family was, as Grace put it,

"lower middle-class," but they were surrounded by the natural features Grace would need to feed her imagination and shape her envi-
ronmentally conscious politics: city lots and coastal beaches. Like
Louisa May Alcott, Grace was a self-described "tomboy." She had
a sister as well as brothers, but in her portrayal of outdoor adven-
tures, Grace is often engaging in strenuous physical activities with
the boys or exploring her environment on her own. In her memoir
Living for Change, Boggs recalled the fenced yard at the side of their
house where she and her brothers threw baseballs and built an ice
hockey rink. When her family began to spend summers in a rented
house on Long Island's South Shore, Grace became a beach lover.
She collected clams and swam competitively alongside her brothers
(and won second place in a local contest). She also rode her bicycle, a
sign of women's growing independence in the 1890s and early 1900s,
all around town. We can imagine the future philosopher on these
humid, summer days, pushing the pedals of her bicycle while she
thought and dreamed in motion. The first book Grace ever owned
was *The Secret Garden*, by Frances Hodgson Burnett, a gift from a
teacher that seems symbolic in hindsight, as Grace would become an
early proponent of the urban garden movement—the kind of growing ground that was, like Burnett's fictionalized spot, tucked behind
walls and inside ignored lots, thriving in unexpected places. By the
time Grace moved to Detroit as a young woman in the early 1950s,
she had read of gardens with the power to transform human relations
and retained a muscle memory of what it felt like to move freely and
exhaustingly outdoors, even as she was keenly aware of the prejudice
against Asian Americans that played out on city streets.

Dolores Huerta, the legendary Mexican American labor activist, was born in New Mexico not long after Boggs was born on

the opposite side of the country. Huerta's relationship to landscape was different from Boggs's, but just as consequential. Huerta was a devoted Girl Scout from 1938 to 1948, from the age of eight to the year of her high school graduation. In the 1940s, Huerta would have gone camping at Lake Alpine and at Camp Menzies in the Sierra Nevadas with Troop 8 of Stockton, California, an unusually diverse group of Girl Scouts in that period, which included Latina, Filipina, Chinese American, African American, and Euro-American youth. On these trips, Huerta would have become familiar with wild lands and park lands, inevitably noting how they were more or less welcoming to different racial populations. It was in the Girl Scouts, Dolores Huerta later wrote, that she learned "how to be strong." Hers was a strength of conviction that other girls, too, acquired outside.

Later, as an adult mother of seven, Dolores Huerta cofounded the National Farm Workers Association, later called the United Farm Workers Union, with Cesar Chavez. Their organization joined with others to mount the 1965 Delano grape strike, a historic action for the advance of farm laborers' rights. Huerta then led a national grape boycott.

While Huerta was advancing a series of national campaigns on behalf of agricultural workers from her post in California, Grace Lee Boggs was engaging in labor organizing and community building in her adopted city of Detroit. Based on her experience on the ground, Boggs helped to shape an inventive community program that would reach people where they lived. In the 1990s, Grace Lee Boggs cofounded Detroit Summer, a youth organization that, among other projects, reanimated city lands, planting what she described in her memoir as "neighborhood gardens, youth gardens, church gardens, school gardens, hospital gardens, senior Independence

gardens, Wellness gardens, Hope Takes Root gardens, and Kwan-
zaa Gardens." The best characterization of this work, Boggs wrote,
was "planting seeds of Hope" because, as she emphasized, "Detroit
is a city of Hope rather than a city of Despair." Grace Lee Boggs
understood the stakes of publicly adopting and beautifying ground,
of working the land in the company of others, and of building urban
environments that cleaved to the natural shape of the earth while
supporting common human needs for nourishment and relationship.
In her endeavors, Boggs insisted on "a sense of history" and routinely
asked of her listeners, "What time is it on the clock of the world?"
But for her, sustainable change could grow gradually over time, like
a seedling in the soil.

*Dolores Huerta wears a woven poncho
and carries a flag as she pickets outside
a D'Agostino's supermarket during a
United Farm Workers campaign.* Photo
by Jacqueline Bernard, 1921–1938. Used
by permission of the Schlesinger Library,
Harvard Radcliffe Institute, Harvard
University.

Like her older contemporaries Dolores Huerta and Grace Lee Boggs, Octavia E. Butler, who was born in 1947 and passed away in 2006, was a nature lover. Casting this orientation of sensory attention outward, Butler developed a sharp analysis of social, cultural, and political challenges (waning democracies, transformative pandemics, space travel), as well as their stakes for humankind, that resonates with national and world events of the twenty-first century. Best known for her science fiction—a genre in which she was the only Black woman publishing consistently for most of her career—Butler achieved critical acclaim and a devoted readership for her wildly imaginative work featuring deep dimensions of the human experience in changed and new worlds. Over the course of her career, Butler won literary prizes and was heralded as the first, and until recent years, only, science fiction writer to win the MacArthur "genius" grant. She was, as well, the first African American to win a MacArthur for fiction writing. According to a fellow writer and interviewer, Randall Kenan, Butler was the most prolific Black woman novelist in North America in the early 1990s, having published twelve novels and several short stories over her lifetime.

Although she resisted categorization and preferred to identify broadly as a writer and storyteller, Butler is viewed as a progenitor of Black speculative fiction and Afrofuturism. Her fearless fiction transcends time and upends expectations, a cutting-edge quality that has made her work increasingly relevant in a rapidly shifting, increasingly anxiety-ridden twenty-first-century world. In 2020, her 1993 novel *Parable of the Sower* made the *New York Times* bestseller list, a dream of Butler's never achieved in her lifetime. In 2020, NASA announced the Octavia E. Butler Landing site on Mars to mark the touchdown site of the rover Perseverance. Butler, who wrote passionately yet critically about the potential for human survival on Earth and on Mars, is heralded now as a philosopher and futurist. Less known is Octavia Butler's concern about and attention to the natural world of planet Earth—the ways in which she is a creative heir to authors like Harriet Jacobs and Mamie Garvin Fields, Black women who wrote about slavery as well as nature and the integral relations between them. Butler was, like them, an environment and climate writer.

Octavia Butler's attachment to the outdoors began when she was a girl living with her mother on her grandmother's chicken ranch in the high desert near present-day Victorville, California. The ranch was a magical place for Butler, where she recalled gazing up at a vast sky, tracking the stars, and gaining perspective about personal standpoint and human social relations, much like the young nineteenth-century abolitionist Laura Smith Haviland had done. And perhaps like enslaved girls who had witnessed the Leonid meteor shower, Butler later said that those desert skies imparted to her the wisdom that there were "parts of the world that human beings don't dominate." Butler's fascination with the stars would lead her into a life of rich imaginings. As a grade schooler in Pasadena, California, Butler penned her first story about a wild horse called Silver Star. She began the story with a night sky setting, writing in looping cursive: "The island shown brightly for it was a full moon it was the night before I was born one star seem to be brighter than all the others all of a sudden it began to fall it landed on my mothers sho[u]lder the next day I was born."

As an adult, Butler kept lists of the flowering plants and trees in her neighborhood, jotting down quick observations, like: "Camphor is golden green blossoming on some streets. On others, bearing; Azelias blooming madly New shoots at the ends of deodar pine branches . . . Camilias—Few, but perfect beautiful." She developed an enduring writing practice that included the outdoors and the scenic range ringing Los Angeles that she called "my mountains," admitting that "the truth is, city woman that I am, they scare me a little." Awaking in the dark of night, Butler would write through the dawn and embark on a daily walk in the cradle of the San Gabriels. When she moved to Seattle in her fifties, Butler fell in love with a tree in her yard and published a short story, "The Book of Martha," about a Black woman writer communing with God near an urban lake.

Octavia Butler was deeply concerned about climate change and saw an inherent conflict between "small sustainable communities" and "the expensive high tech dream of . . . colonizing the stars." Butler was also an environmental defender, working with the Sierra Club on her home ground of Washington State. She told an interviewer, fantasy author and literature scholar Susan Palwick, that she was "horrified" by "the sight of [her] first clear-cut on the side of a hill." The Butler archives at the Huntington Library include a letter penned by Butler to a US president: in 2001, she sent a letter to George W. Bush on Sierra Club letterhead urging environmental protections.

Octavia Butler's tenth novel, *Parable of the Sower*, contends with climate change along with a host of other dire social issues, such as drug abuse, extreme class stratification, sexual exploitation, and modern-day slavery. In an interview with filmmaker Julie Dash

Octavia E. Butler stands outside her home in Seattle, Washington, beside a favorite tree.
Octavia E. Butler Papers, Huntington Library, San Marino, California. Copyright © by Octavia
E. Butler. Reprinted by permission of the Octavia E. Butler Estate.

(acclaimed for *Daughters of the Dust*), Butler remarked that "global
warming is a kind of character in the book." The book's protagonist/
heroine is a Black teenaged girl who saves herself and others by going
outside and braving the open road. When the novel opens, Lauren
Oya Olamina is reflecting on her fifteenth birthday, which arrives
with more anxiety than joy. The adults in Lauren's life have been disoriented by a "plague" that resulted in population collapse, soaring
inflation, and rampant criminality. Her family lives in a settlement
outside of Los Angeles in 2024, when governmental structures, civic
institutions, and municipal services have broken down, wildfires
and human-induced fires rage across landscapes and streetscapes,
and safety only seems possible behind patrolled neighborhood walls.

Tormented by recurring dreams of destruction and a drug-induced disability that makes her especially vulnerable and unnaturally empathetic, Lauren recognizes that her family and community have achieved an illusory security that will not last. She begins to plan for the worst by studying Indigenous plants and foodways, storing seeds, maps, and cash, and packing a doubled pillowcase with these and more emergency items, which she buries beneath a lemon tree in her family's backyard garden. When her neighborhood compound is attacked by brutal arsonists who murder her family and friends, Lauren unearths her hidden sack and flees. Over many months she persists outside, feeding and clothing herself and building relationships with other refugees who have taken to the dangerous, crime-ridden road, including fugitives from neo-slavery who share her condition of hyperempathy, making them desirable as captive laborers.

As the known world ruptures around her, Lauren Olamina, Black girl superhero, matures into the leader of a racially and ethnically diverse tribe. She survives because of the outdoor education of her youth—her grit, smarts, bravery, and respect for nature. Together with her newfound kin, Lauren develops a religion she has invented, called Earthseed, in a community she names Acorn. The teenaged girl whom readers meet at the start of this novel lives in a time of environmental and political collapse. She is forced to choose between the devastation behind the walls of her depleted, if familiar, domestic enclave and the riotous, uncharted world outside. Lauren decides to brave the unknown, to reach for the stars, and in so doing plants a community of hope.

Butler wrote *Parable of the Sower* as a warning about a "grim future," of "the things that we're doing now and the kind of future we're buying for ourselves if we're not careful." She achieved in fictional form the specter of a terrifyingly transformed world that climate writers, scientific reports, daily news coverage, and personal experiences around the globe are presently revealing. As I write these words in the early winter of 2022, one and a half years into the novel coronavirus pandemic and against the backdrop of over-lapping, unprecedented local and global climate shocks (fires, floods, freak storms, mudslides), I see "outside" as Butler described it in Lauren Olamina's coming-of-age story. It is a place where the walls of the known world are crumbling but where alternatives might still be possible if only we are willing to imagine them.

Like Harriet Tubman before us, a "once in a blue moon" vision-ary, we, too, might find the way forward by trusting in trees and wishing on stars.

EPILOGUE: TREE TOPS

THE SEEDS OF this book were planted back in 2008 when I realized Harriet Tubman was a woodswoman. Experiencing the COVID-19 pandemic just over a decade later cast this subject matter into a new light. When spring finally burst into warm bloom in 2020, bringing a sense of relief after the dark start of the new year, my children and I built a fairy village in our front yard for the neighborhood kids to enjoy. I noticed more bird feeders and tomato planters appearing outside of single-family houses, duplexes, and triplexes. I was also struck by a comment on quarantine made by a friendly neighbor with whom I conversed while rolling out the trash and recycling bins. When I asked how their family was doing with the strain of pandemic restrictions, the neighbor said: "It's great to have a big yard." This was an understatement. They had one of the largest yards in the neighborhood, with a double lot, gorgeous old-growth trees, grape vines, tenderly tended vegetable and flower gardens, a rabbit hutch, twinkling fairy lights, and even a water element that flowed in all seasons and had the appearance of a natural spring-fed pond. And I had a big yard, too. Although it was not nearly as large or fanciful as my neighbor's outdoor oasis, our

yard was a boon in those stressful times. It provided green ease for
the eyes, ample tree canopy, a space for individual family members to separate and blow off steam, and a place of respite safe from
the threat of viral contagion (as we all then imagined could readily spread in public outdoor spaces). My neighbor's family and my
family were incredibly advantaged compared with many people in
our city and even on adjacent blocks, as well as most people in other
northeastern cities like New York and Boston being hit hard in
those first waves of the virus's assault. I realized, while absorbing
the full impact of my neighbor's words, that differential access to
outdoor green space in urban areas was stark, and the pandemic was
revealing and magnifying these inequities. I thought especially of
other families with teenagers or toddlers (both being at those special ages of particular challenge) who were boxed up in apartments
and homes with no yards. How were they managing schoolwork
online, homework in tight corners, the spontaneous crying, reck-
less crawling, and dangerous degrees of boredom that the closure of
schools and daycare centers had wrought?

Even as isolation restrictions eased, I saw a troubling link between
the green space inequities revealed by our contemporary pandemic
moment and the study I was by then planning with my editor about
American girls outdoors. I was preparing to argue that time spent
in contemplation and action outside had improved and changed the
lives of these girls, many of whom would later change the nation. It
did not seem a leap to consider that natural surroundings and outside
exploration would be just as important to the well-being and growth
of girls and youth of all genders in the twenty-first century, especially
when such green and "wild" spaces are fewer and farther between
due to urban and agricultural development. Scientific studies have

now shown that romping outside strengthens young people's motor skills, cognitive development, and motivation and offers "unique stimulus" for "the sense of discovery" and "meaningful learning." An interesting added benefit of outdoor play may accrue especially to girls and nonbinary kids, as natural materials and environments "are not gender-coded in the same way as places and artifacts created by humans beings," as one geographer points out. The relatively gender-neutral characteristic of natural areas would suggest that playmates can bring greater flexibility, and therefore greater creativity, to their outdoor imaginings and activities.

The outdoors is clearly essential to our collective health and well-being and especially to children's growth. Yet current research shows how race and economic status can circumscribe access to green spaces. In an article titled "COVID-19 Crisis Demonstrates the Urgent Need for Urban Greenspaces," researchers who noted an increased interest in taking walks outside pointed to the "desire to seek recreation and solace in green settings during times of crisis" and referenced the "well-documented health benefits of exposure to natural environments." Another group of researchers found that tree canopy had a more robust impact than "other forms of urban greenery such as open grass spaces" during the pandemic, writing that "tree-rich greenspace" supported mental health, showing "significant protective effects on both depression and composite mental health scores." Yet tree canopy, in particular, has been linked by forest researchers to social and economic difference and historical bias. Urban forestry advocate Ian Leahy wrote in the *New York Times* in 2021 that "neighborhoods with a majority of people in poverty have 25 percent less tree canopy on average than those with a minority of people in poverty" and that past discriminatory policies like residential redlining

(the cordoning off of certain neighborhoods for downgraded mort-
gage and infrastructure opportunities) are linked to this contemporary green deficit in low-income communities. Neighborhoods with
ample trees were not only more pleasing to the eye, but also as much
as 10 degrees cooler than dense, low-tree, impoverished areas. Just
as alarmingly, researchers studying COVID-19 and the environment found that while spending time in parks was associated with
less emotional stress for college-aged students during the pandemic,
people accessing those parks were more likely to be white. Asian
and Black students generally used parks less often and also reported
poorer health during those months. The authors found that "histor-
ically marginalized communities" had experienced lesser degrees of
park access prior to the public health crisis and speculated that "preexisting disparities in both use of parks and access to parks might be
magnified in the era of COVID-19."

Differential access to outside green space is a long-term issue of
social inequality. If, as this book has argued, going outside exercised
the imagination and strengthened skills for girls of the past, and
if being outside buoys mental health and boosts creativity for kids
in the present, our current spatial arrangements are disadvantaging
some children and teens who need the outdoors to test their mettle,
grow their potential, find peace, and enjoy beauty.

So how can we foster outside equity, inviting all into the wild to
watch the sky, climb a tree, and dream the future?

Walking Trees, by Lucy Jackson, June 2021. *This photograph of trees and vines pushing toward the sky was taken during the second summer of the COVID-19 pandemic by Lucy Jackson, a hiker, nature photographer, and undergraduate researcher who contributed to* Wild Girls. Used by permission of Lucy Jackson.

ACKNOWLEDGMENTS

After becoming a tenured professor in the Department of Afroamerican and African Studies (DAAS) at the University of Michigan and sharing the joy and struggles of raising two young girls, I wanted to shape opportunities for girls in local cities to experience the magic of the outdoors and the deep sense of possibility that going outside and paying attention can yield. In 2011, I founded a project called Environmental and Cultural Opportunities for Girls in Urban Southeast Michigan (ECO Girls) and funded it for seven years through grants from the University of Michigan School of Education and National Center for Institutional Diversity, the Michigan Humanities Council (a state arm of the National Endowment for the Humanities), an alumni women's organization, and a prize from the MacArthur Foundation, and with the use of donated space from the University of Michigan's DAAS and the School for Environment and Sustainability and also the Ann Arbor YMCA.

I developed a curricular philosophy for the ECO Girls program, imagining layers of learning like rich, living soil. Layer 1 prioritized strengthening confidence, creativity, and a sense of community through connections with nature. Layer 2 focused on exposure to green and wild places and to a range of cultural histories rooted in place. Layer 3 was geared toward outdoor skill building and local environmental learning. Layer 4 focused on developing critical consciousness about environmental problems (including overconsumption and climate change) and on exploring creative alternatives that fostered earth stewardship and sustainable, resilient life habits. To improve and enact this curricular vision, I gathered an incredible team of undergraduate and graduate students as well as volunteers from DAAS and the Ann Arbor community. Many of the founding staff members of ECO Girls are working today in higher education, secondary education, and Indigenous community, environmental, and public health advocacy. (For more on the history and mission of ECO Girls: a list of staff members, community partners and funders, as well as a pdf including our projects and curriculum, visit the ECO Girls website: https://environmentforgirls.org/.)

ECO Girls recruited heavily in Detroit, and most of our participants were African American elementary and middle schoolers. A few of the girls were Latina and Asian American, a few were mixed-race, including Native American, and a few were Euro-American. ECO Girls offered a free or low-cost afterschool and weekend program, a summer camp (named Camp Bluestem after a local grass) held on the Ann Arbor campus and at the UM Biological Station at Douglass Lake in northern Michigan, and a one-time Black feminist environmental retreat. ECO Girls events (nature walking, tree tending, tree climbing, garden planting, Earth Day slumber partying, story writing, recipe collecting, place mapping, quilt making, journaling, stargazing, and more) were vibrant, adventurous, and joyous.

The ECO Girls activities that I treasure most combined nature, history, and storytelling. I recall fondly our trip to the Detroit River Park, Belle Isle, and the Great Lakes Dossein Shipwreck Museum and my own spontaneous storytelling inspired by the riverine background. While the children sat on the ground, viewing the river and eating their lunches, I told them about courageous enslaved Black people who had crossed this same Detroit River, often with the aid of others in the community, to seize freedom in Ontario, Canada. There is nothing quite like sharing ground with a circle of young people, telling them things—real things that happened in that very place where they came from—and seeing on their faces, bright and uptilted like sunflowers to the light, that those stories were spirit lifters.

The ECO Girls project was a satisfying, challenging, and time-intensive labor of love. I was so busy running it (and being a faculty member, a departmental chair, and a mother of my own young children) that I did not take time away to reflect on the experience in writing beyond penning much of the text of our extensive website. This Norton series of anniversary shorts has granted me space and encouragement to reflect on the ECO Girls initiative and to write as I might to the girls in that program who are now young women (or perhaps gender nonbinary people or trans men) in their late teens and twenties. It is in the spirit and tone of that riverside chat on Detroit's Belle Isle that I have presented this little book.

Wild Girls is about the past as a time different from our own *and* about how the past can lend insight into the present. The contemporary mood in parts of the book was inspired by the Instagram page of a self-described "Black," "queer, "outdoor gurl" (and, behind the scenes, a trained historic preservationist) named Sarah Scruggs, who posts jaw-dropping photographs of herself hiking trails, scaling cliffs, balancing on rocks, wielding tools, making Black power fists above death-defying drops, and otherwise doing outrageous things in stunningly varied and gorgeous landscapes. Scruggs calls her page "She Trail Ready," a name that captures both defiant attitude and willful action. When I read that expression attached to bold images that made my stomach lurch at the sheer scale and bravery of the enterprise, I thought immediately of Harriet Tubman, whose first steps on the trail rocked many worlds, including her own.

This book would not exist without the inspired suggestion, steady encouragement, and wise editorial hand of Alane Mason, who proposed that I turn my past project on environmental education for girls into words. Tanya McKinnon provided invaluable feedback, as always, and stewarded the book's placement. A Harvard-Radcliffe Institute Fellowship afforded me the time to write, while a Schlesinger Library Long 19th Amendment Grant funded summer research for a course that seeded this book. I was fortunate to have excellent and energetic graduate student research assistants working on this project: Hannah Scruggs, Dylan Nelson, Perri Meldon, and, several years ago when I began cataloging nature motifs in slave narratives, Michelle May-Curry, as well as dedicated and enthusiastic undergraduate research assistants funded by the Schlesinger Library in the summer of 2020 and by Harvard-Radcliffe Institute during my year as a Radcliffe fellow in 2021–2022: Kyra March, Alejandro Eduarte, Orlee Marini-Rapoport, and Lucy Jackson. I am indebted to Taylor Maurice, who conducted research on Louisa May Alcott and the Alcott family gardens on my behalf. I am grateful to the many Radcliffe fellows in my class whose insights helped to refine my ideas, particularly Amy Farrell, Ariela Gross, and Anne

Whiston Spirn. I am also thankful to colleagues and friends who shared theme and craft notes about storytelling, nature, environmental justice and adaptation, and urban environments: Beth James, Kristin Hass, Dorceta Taylor, Kelly Cunningham, Anne Steinert, Susan Kollin, Mary Murphy, Mart Stewart, Lauret Savoy, Connie Chiang, Rosalyn LaPier, Sara St. Antoine, Sunita Dhurandhar, Stephen Gray, Dan Smith, Bruno Carvalho, and Kerri Arsenault and Bathsheba Demuth of the Environmental Storytelling Studio at Brown University. This work was buoyed by the generosity of environmentalist editor Emily Levine, who provided an interview and document with the kind aid of Lynne Allen, and by the Native American studies scholar Brian Klopotek, women's history scholar Elizabeth Cobbs, and environmental writer Lauret Savoy, who carefully read draft chapters and offered instructive, illuminating feedback as well as important corrections. My spouse, Joe Gone (whose family hails from Ft. Belknap), was an indispensable contributor to chapter 3. He traveled with me to the places described, encouraged my interpretation from the beginning, and offered key corrections on the draft. Thank you as well to Justin Cahill and Caroline Adams at Norton and copyeditor Janet Greenblatt, who each contributed important comments, helpful corrections, and logistical assistance.

I owe a deep debt of gratitude to the original staff of ECO Girls, whose creativity and hard work helped turn a sabbatical year notion into a full-fledged weekend program and summer camp Up North: Beth James, Alexandria "Alyx" Cadotte, Zakiyah Sayyed, Mallory Horne, Alexandra "Lili" Passarelli, Rachel Afi Quinn, Tayana Hardin (and anyone whose name may be slipping my mind in the present moment!). I am grateful to the students in my Native women and abolitionist women courses offered at the University of Michigan and Harvard University; their smart and eager responses in class sparked new ideas. I am likewise indebted to the sharp teaching fellows I worked with in these courses at Harvard: Sarah Sadlier, Camara Brown, and Alyssa Napier, and to Beth Eby, whose guest presentation in my class broadened my knowledge of girls' sports in boarding schools. My extended family remains my guiding night-sky constellation, and I am nostalgically thankful to my cousin Alice, who always listened. I have misty memories of my twins, Blue Bird and Alley Cat, members of the original ECO Girls as grade schoolers, and of their sibling, Silver Fox, who was a preschooler at the time and sometimes got to tag along. Sun Old Man, you remain my steadfast traveling companion across the byways of Montana and the world.

NOTES ON SOURCES AND QUOTATIONS

PREFACE: ICE BRIDGES

For the Ohio River's name and freezing cycles, I relied on the following sources. The entry "American Indians in Ohio" attributes the word
"Ohio" to Seneca, defined as "it is beautiful," in Native Languages of
the Americas, http://www.native-languages.org/ohio.htm. "Ohio River"
(or *Ohiyo*), meaning "beautiful river," New World Encyclopedia, http://
www.newworldencyclopedia.org/entry/Ohio_River. The following source
gives the Iroquois meaning as "great river": "Ohio River," Ohio History Central, http://www.ohiohistorycentral.org/w/Ohio_River. David White, Karla
Johnston, Michael Miller, "Ohio River Basin," in Arthur C. Benke and Col-
bert E. Cushing., eds., *Rivers of North America* (Amsterdam: Elsevier Academic
Press, 2005), 375. The National Weather Service lists 1917–18 as the coldest
winter on record in the Ohio River area and 1977–78 as the second coldest winter on record. In 1977–78, cold weather resulted in power outages and school
closures for nearly a month. "Ohio River Freeze," National Weather Service,
www.weather.gov/lmk/ohio_river_freeze. Kristina Goetz, "Don't Look for
River to Freeze over Soon," *Cincinnati Enquirer*, December 31, 2000. Billy
Davis, "Frozen Ohio River, January 1977," *Courier Journal*, *USA Today*, January
6, 2014. The National Weather Service (same article as above) dates the first
freeze of the Ohio River to 1856 and the last freeze to 1977–78. The Mississippi
River also has a history of freezing. Tim O'Neil, "1936: When the Mississippi
River Froze Over," *St. Louis Dispatch*, February 6, 2017. Most contemporary
newspaper accounts mention Mississippi River freezes in the mid-1800s and
especially in the late 1800s and early 1900s.

For Margaret Garner's history, I consulted the sources that follow. Nikki M. Taylor, *Driven Toward Madness: The Fugitive Slave Margaret Garner and Tragedy on the Ohio* (Athens: Ohio University Press, 2016). Delores M. Walters, "Introduction: Re(dis)covering and Recreating the Cultural Milieu of Margaret Garner, in Mary E. Frederickson and Delores M. Walters, eds., *Gendered Resistance: Women, Slavery, and the Legacy of Margaret Garner* (Urbana: University of Illinois Press, 2013). "The Slave Case in Cincinnati," *The National Anti-Slavery Standard*, February 16, 1856. "Delivery of the Cincinnati Slaves at Covington," *The Liberator*, March 7, 1856. "The Case of the Slave Mother, Margaret, at Cincinnati," *The Liberator*, May 16, 1856. "Stampede of Slaves," *Chicago Tribune*, January 28, 1856. "Negro Stampede," *Covington Journal*, as cited by Weisenburger, *Modern Medea.* Steven Weisenburger, *Modern Medea: A Family Story of Slavery and Child-Murder from the Old South* (New York: Hill and Wang, 1998). "The Slave Case in Cincinnati," *The National Anti-Slavery Standard*, February 16, 1856. "Delivery of the Cincinnati Slaves at Covington," *The Liberator*, March 7, 1856. The Garner story has been retold in poetry, fiction, film, and opera; for example: Toni Morrison, *Beloved* (New York: Plume, 1987); Richard Danielpour and Toni Morrison, "Notes on Margaret Garner," Cincinnati Opera 2005 Summer Festival program (Cincinnati: Cincinnati Opera, 2005), 20–21. I write about Harper's poetry and Garner's flight in the forthcoming piece: Tiya Miles, "'Bright Visions of Deliverance': Black Women's Space-Making through Stories," environmental justice and storytelling forum, *Journal of Environmental History*, 2023.

For Harper's poetry, I consulted: Frances Ellen Watkins Harper, *A Brighter Coming Day: A Frances Ellen Watkins Harper Reader*, ed. Frances Smith Foster (New York: Feminist Press, 1990); Melba Joyce Boyd, *Discarded Legacy: Politics and Poetics in the Life of Frances E. W. Harper, 1825–1911* (Detroit: Wayne State University Press, 1994); Kristine Yohe, "Enslaved Women's Resistance and Survival Strategies in Frances Ellen Watkins Harper's 'The Slave Mother: A Tale of the Ohio,' and Toni Morrison's *Beloved* and Margaret Garner," in Mary E. Frederickson and Delores M. Walters, eds., *Gendered Resistance: Women, Slavery, and the Legacy of Margaret Garner* (Urbana: University of Illinois Press, 2013).

Rutherford B. Hayes was interviewed by Wilbur H. Siebert, Spring 1893, Wilbur H. Siebert Underground Railroad Collection: The Underground Railroad in Ohio: Hamilton County series IV, vol. 7.

INTRODUCTION: WAY FINDERS

As a child, I unknowingly engaged in a process that the landscape historian John Stilgoe has called exploration of our "everyday landscapes." In *Outside Lies Magic*, Stilgoe argues that engaging in and with the world outdoors, defined as "the whole concatenation of wild and artificial things, the natural ecosystem as modified by people over the centuries, the built environment layered over layers," leads to the expansion of "any mind focused on it." John R. Stilgoe, *Outside Lies Magic: Regaining History and Awareness in Everyday Places* (New York: Walker and Company, 1998), 1, 2.

For the epigraph quotes, see Carolyn Finney, "Who Gets Left Out of the 'Great Outdoors' Story?" *New York Times*, November 4, 2021; Ashley E. Remer and Tiffany R. Isselhardt, *Exploring American Girlhood through 50 Historic Treasures* (London: Rowman and Littlefield, 2021), xiii. Readers may wonder about the absence of the Girl Scouts and Campfire Girls in this book. Because this is a short book and those organizations have complex histories regarding race, including the appropriation and misrepresentation of Native American practices as well as discriminatory and ethically compromised procedures, I opted not to focus on them.

CHAPTER 1: STAR GAZERS

Tubman's weed quote comes from Benjamin Drew, *The Narratives of Fugitive Slaves in Canada* (1856; reprint, Toronto: Coles Publishing Company, 1972), 30. For recent biographies and studies of Tubman, I relied on and at times quoted from: Kate Clifford Larson, *Harriet Tubman: Bound for the Promised Land* (New York: One World Random House, 2004), 29, 32; Catherine Clinton, *Harriet Tubman: The Road to Freedom* (New York: Back Bay Books, 2005), 20, 37; Lois E. Horton, *Harriet Tubman and the Fight for Freedom: A Brief History with Documents* (Boston: Bedford/St. Martin's, 2013); Jean M. Humez, *Harriet Tubman: The Life and the Life Stories* (Madison: University of Wisconsin Press, 2003), 6; Erica Armstrong Dunbar, *She Came to Slay: The Life and Times of Harriet Tubman* (New York: Simon and Schuster, 2019), 23; Deirdre Cooper Owens, "Harriet Tubman's Disability and Why It Matters," *Ms. Magazine*, February 10, 2022, Harriet Tubman Bicentennial Project; Chanda Prescod-Weinstein, "Harriet Tubman, Astronomer Extraordinaire," *Ms. Magazine*, February 3, 2022, Harriet Tubman Bicentennial Project; Janell Hobson, "Karen V. Hill,

Director of the Harriet Tubman Home: She Was Able to Separate the Brutality of Slavery from How She Loved the Land," *Ms. Magazine*, March 2, 2022, Harriet Tubman Bicentennial Project; Allison Keyes, "Harriet Tubman, an Unsung Naturalist, Used Owl Calls as a Signal on the Underground Railroad," *Audubon Magazine*, February 25, 2020. For nineteenth-century biographies of Tubman, I drew from: Sarah H. Bradford, *Harriet Tubman—The Moses of Her People* (1886, 2nd ed.; reprint, Amazon.com); Emma P. Telford, "Harriet, the Modern Moses of Heroism and Visions," Collection of the Cayuga Museum of History and Art, Auburn, New York.

For tree details, I used Sweet Gum, Education- Plants, Maryland Department of Planning, Jefferson Paterson Park and Museum, https://jefpat.maryland.gov/Pages/education/plants/sweet-gum.aspx. Kate Larson points out the danger of these trees and the irony of their use for Tubman's cradle, xiii. For woods lore I read James H. Merrell, *Into the American Woods: Negotiators on the Pennsylvania Frontier* (New York: W.W. Norton, 1999), 22–23.

For Kate Drumgoold's narrative, see Kate Drumgoold, *A Slave Girl's Story: Being an Autobiography of Kate Drumgoold*, Documenting the American South, University of North Carolina Library, docsouth.unc.edu.

For meteor shower/stars falling material, I consulted the sources that follow. Angela Walton-Raji, "The Night the Stars Fell: My Search for Amanda Young," "Getting Started in African American Genealogy," "Freedmen of the Frontier: African American Historical and Genealogical Resource Page of the City of Ft. Smith Arkansas," http://myancestorsname.blogspot.com/2010/04/night-stars-fell-my-search-for-amanda.html. "Aunt Harriet Was Very Old," *Auburn Daily Advertiser*, Auburn, NY, March 12, 1913. Kate Larson discusses this passage as well as other Marylanders' reactions to the meteor shower; Larson, *Harriet Tubman*, 41. Scientists estimate the number of stars in motion that evening at between 50,000 and 150,000. Mary L. Kwas, "The Spectacular 1833 Leonid Meteor Storm: The View from Arkansas," *Arkansas Historical Quarterly* 58, no. 3 (Autumn 1999): 314–324, https://earthsky.org/todays-image/leonid-meteor-shower-1833. "Jane Clark," by Julia C. Ferris, read at the banquet of the Cayuga County Historical Society, February 22, 1897. Jane Clark's former name during her enslavement was Charlotte Harris. I am grateful to Robin Bernstein, who found and transcribed this narrative and shared a copy before publishing it in *Common-Place: The Journal of Early American Life,* common-place.org. Brian Klopotek points out that the year 1833 is also the start date of Native American "winter count" pictographic record keeping on the plains. Gus Bradshaw, quoting a woman he calls Maria, WPA Slave Narratives, Texas, Part 1, www.loc.gov/itemmesn161/, pp. 130–131. Wesley Jones, WPA Slave Narratives, South Carolina, Part 3, www.loc.gov/item/mesn143/, p. 72. Rachel Bradley, WPA Slave Narratives, Arkansas, Part 1, www.loc.gov/item/mesn021/, p. 233. Peter Brown, WPA Slave Narratives, Arkansas, Part 1, www.loc.gov/item/mesn021/, p. 311. See also, regarding speakers marking their ages at this moment: Lewis Evans, WPA Slave Narratives, South Carolina, Part 2, www.loc.gov/item/mesn142/, p. 30, and William Davis, WPA Slave Narratives, Texas, Part 1, www.loc.gov/itemmesn161/, p. 290. Lillie Baccus, WPA Slave Narratives, Arkansas, Part 1, www.loc.gov/item/mesn021/, p. 76. Charlotte Foster, WPA Slave Narratives, South Carolina, Part 2, www.loc.gov/item/mesn142/, p. 83. Betty Hodge, WPA Slave Narratives, Arkansas, Part 3, www.loc.gov/item/mesn023/, pp. 282–283. William Davis also reported end-of-the-world fears; William Davis, WPA Slave Narratives, Texas, Part 1, p. 290. Lizzie Johnson, WPA Slave Narratives, Arkansas, Part 4, www.loc.gov/item/mesn024/, p. 103. Elizabeth Brannon, WPA Narratives, Arkansas, Part 1, www.loc.gov/item/mesn021/, p. 237. Richard Caruthers, WPA Narratives, Texas, Part 1, www.loc.gov/itemmesn161/, p. 199. Museum of Fine Arts, Boston, Harriet Powers Object Files.

For Jacobs, I used and quoted from Harriet A. Jacobs, *Incidents in the Life of a Slave Girl, Written by Herself* (1861; reprint, Cambridge, MA: Harvard University Press, 1987). Katherine McKittrick has analyzed this environmental aspect of Jacobs's writing. Katherine McKittrick, *Demonic Grounds: Black Women and the Cartographies of Struggle* (Minneapolis: University of Minnesota Press, 2006), 37–45, 59–62. Space did not afford a thorough citation of old and new works in Black ecologies and geographies here. I invite readers to keep an eye out for my biography of Harriet Tubman (in progress). As the discussion in this chapter indicates, woods (six appearances) and trees (seven appearances) are the most frequently mentioned natural features in the Jacobs narrative. For Jacobs quotes in this chapter in order of appearance, see pp. 6, 57, 88, 64, 67, 158, 29, 158, 122.

For Haviland quotes, see Laura S. Haviland, *A Woman's Life-Work, Labors and Experiences* (1881; reprint, HardPress, 2016), 9, 10. For background on the production of Haviland's memoir, see Tiya Miles, "'Shall Woman's Voice Be

Hushed?': Laura Smith Haviland in Abolitionist Women's History," *Michigan Historical Review* 39, no. 2 (Fall 2013): 1–20, footnote 20. Delia Webster, a white Vermonter, graduate of Oberlin College, and staunch abolitionist, attempted a Southern rescue in Lexington Kentucky in 1844. Because she did this in partnership with the male abolitionist Calvin Fairbank, her action differs from Haviland's solo attempt. For more on Webster, see Randolph Paul Runyon and William Albert Davis, *Delia Webster and the Underground Railroad* (Lexington: University Press of Kentucky, 1996), 1–3. For Haviland's diary, see: Miles, "Shall Woman's Voice Be Hushed?" 4; Haviland Diary, June 19, 1890, Lenawee County Historical Society Museum, Adrian, MI.

Regarding the final quotation: Frederick Douglass said these words about Tubman in a testimonial for Sarah Bradford's Tubman biography.

CHAPTER 2: NATURE WRITERS

Information about the Orchard House tour comes from an email exchange April 11, 2022, with Taylor Maurice, a staff member from 2008 to 2019 at Louisa May Alcott's Orchard House in Concord, Massachusetts. Information about the family gardens comes from John Matteson, "'I Have a Religion in this Business': Bronson Alcott and the Gardens of Hillside and Orchard House," Lecture, Concord Historical Collaborative Series, Concord, Massachusetts, September 21, 2008, courtesy of Orchard House, collected by Taylor Maurice. Lizzie Alcott, Journal, 1846, courtesy of Orchard House, collected by Taylor Maurice.

For primary and contemporaneous accounts of Louisa May Alcott's life, I drew and quoted from the following sources. Maria S. Porter, "Recollections of Louisa May Alcott" (1892) in Daniel Shealy, *Alcott in Her Own Time: A Biographical Chronicle of Her Life* (Boise: University of Iowa Press, 2005), 58–59. Louisa M. Alcott, "Reflections of My Childhood," in Louisa May Alcott, *Little Women or Meg, Jo, Beth and Amy*, a Norton Critical Edition, ed. Anne K. Phillips and Gregory Eiselein (New York: W. W. Norton, 2004). "Little Red Shoes," clippings, Louisa May Alcott Additional Papers, 1839–1888, MS A, m 2114, Houghton Library, Harvard University (HLHU). Bronson Alcott to Louisa May Alcott, June 21, 1840, Alcott Papers, HLHU. *Daily News*, clippings, Alcott Papers, HLHU. "Conversations," clippings, Alcott Papers, HLHU.

For recent biographical and critical work on Alcott, I consulted and quoted from: John Matteson, "Introduction: Little Pilgrims," in Louisa May Alcott, *The Annotated Little Women*, ed. John Matteson (New York: W. W. Norton, 2016), xiii; John Matteson, "We Really Lived Most of It," in Louisa May Alcott, *The Annotated Little Women*, ed. John Matteson (New York: W. W. Norton, 2016), xxi, xliii, lxviii. And also, Susan Cheever, *Louisa May Alcott: A Personal Biography* (New York: Simon and Schuster, 2010), 21, 78, 43, 85–86, 179, 203, 179, 236.

For the cultural history of the tomboy, I consulted and quoted from Renée M. Sentilles, *American Tomboys, 1850–1915* (Amherst: University of Massachusetts Press, 2018). (Sentilles, Kindle location: 442, 453, 485, 544, 555, 585, 1216, 1227, 1238, 1289–1300, 1352.) Sentilles points out that it was not until the very late nineteenth century and early twentieth century that the tomboy figure took on an ambiguous aspect of "sexuality and gender inversion." The women's skirts quote comes from Remer and Isselhardt, *Exploring American Girlhood*, 66.

Henry David Thoreau mentions an "Indian" basket seller in Concord in the 1840s. Henry David Thoreau, *Walden Pond; or, Life in the Woods* (New York: Thomas Y. Crowell & Company, 1910), 22. See also Daniel Mandell, *Tribe, Race History: Native Americans in Southern New England, 1789–1880* (Baltimore: Johns Hopkins University Press, 2008), 21–25, 243, note 79. Elise Lemire argues, "Some of our nation's cherished green spaces began as black spaces, with Walden Woods a striking case in point." Elise Lemire, *Black Walden: Slavery and Its Aftermath in Concord Massachusetts* (Philadelphia: University of Pennsylvania Press, 2009), 9–11.

For the Alcott-Tubman link, the Boston fundraiser, and the two racial stories, I drew from Humez, *Harriet Tubman*, 41, 364, notes 64, 65. For the Concord visit I drew from Kate Clifford Larson, *Harriet Tubman: Bound for the Promised Land* (New York: One World Random House, 2003), 170. Sarah Elbert notes that Alcott expressed her admiration of Harriet Beecher Stowe's *Uncle Tom's Cabin* in her journals. Elbert also connects Alcott's publication of the abolitionist story "M.L." in the early 1860s to John Brown's failed raid at Harper's Ferry, Virginia, in 1859. Sarah Elbert, "Introduction," in *Louisa May Alcott on Race, Sex, and Slavery*, ed. Sarah Elbert (Boston: Northeastern

University Press, 1997), xxiv. Alcott's novel *Work*, published in 1873, included an African American cook as a minor character. Alcott used dialect for the cook's speech. She also used other characters to criticize white service workers' racial prejudice toward the cook. Humez cites Alcott biographer Martha Saxton's assertion that this (stereotypically drawn) character in *Work* was "unfortunately" modeled on Tubman and was "dismayingly sentimental." Martha Saxton, *Louisa May Alcott: A Modern Biography* (1977; New York: Farrar, Straus, Giroux, 1995), 240. For my reading of *Little Women*, I quoted from two editions. Louisa May Alcott, *Little Women or Meg, Jo, Beth and Amy*, a Norton Critical Edition. ed. Anne K. Phillips and Gregory Eiselein (New York: W. W. Norton, 2004), 11–14, 23, 32, 11–14, 23, 32. Louisa May Alcott, *Little Women*, Vintage Classics (New York: Random House, 2019), 6, 42, 122, 247, 170–171.

For Schoolcraft's poetry, I consulted and quoted from Robert Dale Parker, ed., *The Sound the Stars Make Rushing through the Sky: The Writings of Jane Johnston Schoolcraft* (Philadelphia: University of Pennsylvania Press, 2007), 30, 32, 38. For more on the Johnston women and family, see Emily MacGillivray, "Indigenous Trading Women of the Borderland Great Lakes, 1740 to 1845," PhD diss., University of Michigan, Ann Arbor, 2017.

For Pocahontas's multiple names and her biography, I consulted: Camilla Townsend, *Pocahontas and the Powhatan Dilemma* (New York: Hill and Wang, 2004); Helen C. Rountree, "Pocahontas: The Hostage Who Became Famous," in *Sifters: Native American Women's Lives*, ed. Theda Perdue (New York: Oxford University Press, 2001). Sacagawea's/Sacajawea's name has been rendered with variable spellings and pronunciations. Tribal members, documentary editors, and historians have all considered whether Sacagawea's name originates from the Shoshone language or from the Hidatsa language. "Sakakawea" derives from the Hidatsa language and translates as "Bird Woman." The Mandan-Hidatsa-Arikara nations of the Fort Berthold Reservation (also known as the Three Affiliated Tribes) use the "k" spelling, although "Sacagawea" spelled with a "g" has been widely adopted. The name has also been spelled with a "j." According to the US Forest Service Lewis and Clark Interpretive Center along the National Park Service Lewis and Clark Trail, the common spelling "Sacajawea" is due to a misspelling in an 1814 edition of the Lewis and Clark journals edited by Nicholas Biddle. According to April Summitt, preference for "j" is a Shoshone spelling that alters the translation of the name from "Bird Woman" to "Boat Pusher." Sources I consulted: James P. Ronda, *Lewis and Clark among the Indians* (Lincoln: University of Nebraska Press, 1984); April R. Summitt, *Sacagawea: A Biography* (Westport, CT: Greenwood Press, 2008); Lewis and Clark Interpretive Center exhibition panel, "Sacagawea: The Woman Behind the Myth," Great Falls, MT, October 2021.

For Dye's life and writing, I consulted and quoted: Eva Emery Dye, *The Conquest: The Story of Lewis and Clark* (Chicago: A. C. McClurg & Company, 1902), 228, 251, 242; Sheri Bartlett Browne, *Eva Emery Dye: Romance with the West*, (Corvallis, OR: Oregon State University Press, 2004), 50, 251, 242. For the Indian princess image, see Rayna Green, "The Pocahontas Perplex: The Image of Indian Women in American Culture," *Massachusetts Review* 16, no. 4 (Autumn 1975): 698–714. For a discussion of Sacagawea and cultural imagery, see Chris Finley, "Violence, Genocide, and Captivity: Exploring Cultural Representations of Sacajawea as a Universal Mother of Conquest," *American Indian Cultures and Research Journal* 35, no. 4 (January 2011): 191–208. For suffrage movement figures, I relied on and quoted from Cathleen D. Cahill, *Recasting the Vote: How Women of Color Transformed the Suffrage Movement* (Chapel Hill: University of North Carolina Press, 2020), 22. For more on Dye's and other suffragists' strategic representations of Sacagawea, see Patricia Vettel-Becker, "Sacagawea and Son: The Visual Construction of America's Maternal Feminine," *American Studies* 50, no. 1/2 (2009): 27–50.

For secondary material on *Zitkála-Šá*, I relied on: Kiara M. Vigil, *Indigenous Intellectuals: Sovereignty, Citizenship, and the American Imagination, 1880–1930* (New York: Cambridge University Press, 2015), 166–168; Susan Rose Dominguez, "Zitkála-Šá: The Representative Indian," Introduction, in *Zitkála-Šá, American Indian Stories*, ed. Susan Rose Dominguez (1921; reprint, Lincoln: University of Nebraska Press, 2003); and Cahill's *Recasting the Vote*, 20–21. The primary material on Zitkála-Šá comes from her essays, which I paraphrased and quoted, primarily: "School Days," *American Indian Stories* (1921; reprint, Lincoln: University of Nebraska Press, 2003), 78–79. Regarding Ida B. Wells, I drew from: Dorothy Sterling, *Black Foremothers: Three Lives*, 2nd ed. (New York: Feminist Press, 1988), 109–110; Martha Jones, *Vanguard: How Black Women Broke Barriers, Won the Vote, and Insisted on Equality for All* (New York: Basic Books, 2020), 165.

For Cooper, I referenced: Anna Julia Cooper, *A Voice from the South* (1892; reprint, New York: Oxford University Press, 1988); Mary Helen Washington, "Introduction," in Anna Julia Cooper, *A Voice from the South*, xxvii. Louise Daniel Hutchinson, *Anna J. Cooper, a Voice from the South* (A&I Building-2280, Washington, DC 20560: Published for the Anacostia Neighborhood Museum of the Smithsonian Institution by the Smithsonian Institution Press, 1981), 126, 127, 185 (brochure image). Jones, *Vanguard*, 143–146. Like the Girl Scouts organization, founded by Juliette Gordon Low as the Girl Guides in 1912, the Camp Fire Girls, founded in 1911 by a male doctor, adopted inaccurate approximations of Native American dress, customs, and terms to signal a primordial domesticity for participants. Because records of Cooper's DC chapter have not been uncovered, it is unclear whether she followed this practice. For more on these national girl groups, see: Susan A. Miller, *Growing Girls: The Natural Origins of Girls' Organizations in America* (New Brunswick, N.J.: Rutgers University Press, 2007), 5, 15–16, 18–21; Camp Fire Girls, *The Book of the Camp Fire Girls: With Illustrations* (New York: Camp Fire Girls National Headquarters, 1922); a forthcoming history of the Girl Scouts by Amy Farrell (University of North Carolina Press). Cooper's club combined the education of Black girls with outing activities; it may also have appropriated Native symbols and dress, a hallmark of white Camp Fire Girls clubs. Cooper's political writing indicates, however, that she was sensitive to negative representations of Native people. For a discussion of Anna Julia Cooper's reference to "Indians" in *A Voice from the South*, where she urges white women to fight not only for themselves, but for all women, see Cahill, *Recasting the Vote*, 19.

In the sections on Mamie Garvin Fields, I drew and quoted from: Mamie Garvin Fields with Karen Fields, *Lemon Swamp and Other Places: A Carolina Memoir* (New York: The Free Press, 1983), 9, 67, 80, 81; Toni Morrison, "The Site of Memory," in *What Moves at the Margins: Selected Nonfiction*, ed. Carolyn C. Denard (Jackson: University of Mississippi Press, 2008), 77. For more on Audre Lorde as a nature writer, see Alexis Pauline Gumbs, "Water and Stone: A Ceremony for Audre Lorde in Three Parts," in *A Darker Wilderness: Black Nature Writing from Soil to Stars*, ed. Erin Sharkey (Minneapolis: Milkweed Editions, 2023).

Additional studies on environmental literary ancestors include: Kimberly N. Ruffin, *Black on Earth: African American Ecoliterary Traditions* (Athens: University of Georgia Press, 2010); Jeffrey Myers, *Converging Stories: Race, Ecology, and Environmental Justice in American Literature* (Athens: University of Georgia Press, 2005).

CHAPTER 3: GAME CHANGERS

Cooper quotations come from Cooper, *A Voice from the South*, 78, 117–118, 69.

To reconstruct the history of Fort Shaw women's basketball, I drew primarily on and quoted from the only full-length academic study of the Fort Shaw team: Linda Peavy and Ursula Smith, *Full-Court Quest: The Girls from Fort Shaw Indian School Basketball Champions of the World* (Norman: University of Oklahoma Press, 2008). A Montana Public Television documentary, *Playing for the World*, was based on the book and released in 2010. I also consulted separate chapters by Peavy and Smith: Linda Peavy and Ursula Smith, "Chapter 6. Leav[ing] the White[s] . . . Far Behind Them," in *The 1904 Anthropology Days and Olympic Games*, ed. Susan Brownell (Lincoln: University of Nebraska Press, 2008); Linda Peavy and Ursula Smith, "Unlikely Champion: Emma Rose Sansaver, 1884–1925," in *Portraits of Women in the American West*, ed. Dee Garceau-Hagen (New York: Routledge, 2005). Another book about the team offers a loosely researched treatment: Happy Jack Feder, *"Shoot Minnie, Shoot!" The Story of the 1904 Fort Shaw Indian Girls* (Augusta, MT: Big Sky Stories, 2004). Newspaper coverage that I read about the team included: "Shoot, Minnie, Shoot! Famous Battle Cry Carried Ft. Shaw Indian Belles to 1904 World's Title," reproduced in Daisy (the author of this text is attributed simply as "Daisy"), *An Indian School Diary*, Montana Historical Society, Helena, MT (hereafter MHS); *Great Falls Daily Leader*, November 17, 1902 (as quoted in Peavy and Smith, *Full-Court,* 149, 406, note 5); coverage reproduced in Ken Robison, "'Like a Wall of Fire through a Cane Break': The 1903 Fort Shaw Indian School Girls' Basketball Team Sweeps through Northern Montana," Historical Fort Benton, Joel F. Overholser Historical Research Center, Fort Benton, January 15, 2007, in the *Fort Benton River Press*, January 17, 2007.

The boundaries of the present-day Fort Belknap Reservation were fixed in 1887; the original Fort Belknap had been farther north across the Milk River. For histories of Fort Belknap I drew from: Fort Belknap Reservation Timeline, Montana Office of Public Instruction, 2017, https://opi.mt.gov/Portals/182/

Page%20Files/Indian%20Education/Social%20Studies/K-12%20Resources/
Fort%20Belknap%20Timeline.pdf; "About the Fort Belknap Indian Reservation," Fort Belknap Indian Community, https://ftbelknap.org/; Regina Flannery, *The Gros Ventres of Montana: Part I Social Life* (Washington DC: The Catholic University of America Press, 1953; reprint, 1975); Loretta Fowler, *Shared Symbols, Contested Meanings: Gros Ventre Culture and History, 1778–1984* (Ithaca: Cornell University Press, 1987); S. Doc. No. 117, 54th Cong., 1st Sess. (1896), Letter from the Secretary of the Interior, Transmitting an Agreement Made and Concluded October 9, 1895, with the Indians of the Fort Belknap Reservation, in Montana, by William C. Pollock, George Bird Grinnell, and Walter M. Clements, Commissioners. For the Indian removal era summary, I turned to Claudio Saunt, *Unworthy Republic: The Dispossession of Native Americans and the Road to Indian Territory* (New York: W. W. Norton, 2020).

For context and details of boarding school history, I consulted and at times quoted from the texts that follow. Jon Reyhner and Jeanne Eder, *American Indian Education: A History* (Norman: University of Oklahoma Press, 2004), 151, 191. David Wallace Adams, *Education for Extinction: American Indians and the Boarding School Experience, 1875–1928* (Lawrence: University Press of Kansas, 1995; 2nd edition 2020), 64. K. Tsianina Lomawaima, *They Called It Prairie Light: The Story of Chilocco Indian School* (Lincoln: University of Nebraska Press, 1994), 36, 73, 81. K. Tsianina Lomawaima and Teresa L. McCarty, "Revisiting and Clarifying the Safety Zone," *Journal of American Indian Education* 53, no. 3 (2014): 63–67, 63. Margaret D. Jacobs, *Settler Colonialism, Maternalism, and the Removal of Indigenous Children in the American West and Australia, 1880–1940* (Lincoln: University of Nebraska Press, 2011), xxxii, 151–163. Brenda J. Child and Brian Klopotek, "Introduction: Comparing Histories of Education for Indigenous Peoples," in *Indian Subjects: Hemispheric Perspectives on the History of Indigenous Education*, ed. Brenda J. Child and Brian Klopotek (Santa Fe, NM: School for Advanced Research Press, 2014), 4. Brenda J. Child, "The Boarding School as Metaphor," in *Indian Subjects: Hemispheric Perspectives on the History of Indigenous Education*, ed. Brenda J. Child and Brian Klopotek (Santa Fe, NM: School for Advanced Research Press, 2014), 268. Brenda J. Child, "Boarding Schools," in *Encyclopedia of North American Indians*, ed. Frederick E. Hoxie (Boston: Houghton Mifflin Company, 1996), 79–80. Kim Cary Warren, *The Quest for Citizenship: African American and Native American Education in Kansas, 1880–1935* (Chapel Hill: University of North Carolina Press, 2010), 64, 76, 91. For more on how boarding school policy was also a land extraction policy, see Brenda J. Child, "US Boarding Schools for Indians Had a Hidden Agenda," *Washington Post*, August 27, 2021. My treatment of Gertrude Bonnin's boarding school experience draws, as in chapter 2, from Vigil, *Indigenous Intellectuals*; Dominguez, "Zitkála-Šá: The Representative Indian"; Zitkála-Šá, "Indian Childhood" and "An Indian Teacher," in *American Indian Stories* (1921; reprint, Lincoln: University of Nebraska Press, 2003), 21–22.

While I have not done the research necessary to claim this difference between white fathers and Native mothers as a definitive pattern, I note it in the Fort Shaw team's history. Susan Wirth (Woman That Kills Wood), of the Fort Peck Reservation, was against sending her children to Fort Shaw, but her husband made the decision with the Indian Agent. Her daughter, Nettie Wirth, would become a member of the basketball team. (Peavy and Smith, *Full-Court*, 28–29, 40.)

In the northern plains, some women hunted with their male relatives. See Nancy Bonvillain, "Gender Relations in Native North America," *American Indian Culture and Research Journal* 13, no. 2 (1989): 1–28. There is also evidence of a small number of females taking up male lifestyles and becoming hunters. See the biography of Woman Chief, a natal Gros Ventre woman taken captive by and adopted by the Crows in the late 1800s. Woman Chief became a successful hunter and warrior. See, Edwin Thompson Denig, *Five Tribes of the Upper Missouri*, ed. John C. Ewers (Norman: University of Oklahoma Press, 1975), 195–200. Women accompanied men on communal hunts, but their involvement decreased over time as horses became more plentiful, reducing the need for larger hunting parties. Martha Foster has argued that Crow and Hidatsa wives maintained control over meat distribution after hunting became more male-centric and individualized because men immediately relinquished the meat to women. See Martha Harroun Foster, "Of Baggage and Bondage: Gender and Status among Hidatsa and Crow Women," *American Indian Culture and Research Journal* 17, no. 2 (1993): 121–152.

For the section on Sacagawea, I drew heavily from Elizabeth A. Fenn, *Encounters at the Heart of the World: A History of the Mandan People* (New York: Hill and Wang, 2014), 215–218; and April R. Summitt, *Sacagawea: A Biography* (Westport, CT: Greenwood Press, 2008), 3, 6, 8, 13, 16. I also consulted and quoted from: Ronda, *Lewis and Clark*, xxvi, 6, 7, 135; Walter Johnson, *The Broken Heart of America: St. Louis and the Violent History of the United States*

(New York: Basic Books, 2020), 22; Rowena McClinton, "Background to the Corps of Discovery Encounters with Sacagawea," Missouri History Museum, Forest Park, St. Louis, MO, June 21, 2018, 2. I drew on Laura E. Donaldson, "Red Woman, White Dreams: Searching for Sacagawea," *Feminist Studies*, 32, no. 3 (Fall 2006): 523–533. Charbonneau was born in 1759; he would have been approximately forty-three when he acquired Sacagawea. Weak primary documentation on exactly how Charbonneau attained Sacagawea leads to interpretive gaps. According to Fenn, men in the Mandan and Hidatsa villages were apparently aware that women, particularly physically appealing women, could bring high prices from European traders. Expedition entries are quoted from *Journals of the Lewis and Clark Expedition* (JLCE), University of Nebraska Lincoln, August 14, 1805, JLCE, July 13, 1806, lewisandclarkjournals.unl.edu.

For details on the Sun River environment and the military history of the area, I read and quoted Rosalyn R. LaPier, *Invisible Reality: Storytellers, Storytakers, and the Supernatural World of the Blackfeet* (Lincoln: University of Nebraska Press, 2017), 46. La Pier notes that reservation life limited women's ability to gather plants a distance away; this led to certain plants being even more prized and the increased trading among women plant collectors. I also read Rosalyn LaPier, "Land as Text: Learning to Read Landscape," environmental justice and storytelling forum, *Journal of Environmental History* (forthcoming, Spring 2023). For the local history of the school and the military presence and spatial organization of the post, I drew from: Nan Cole and the English Department of the Fort Shaw High School, *The History of Fort Shaw*, MHS, 1936–1937; Sun River Project, Montana Fort Shaw Indian School Site, March 11, 1914, MHS. *The History of Fort Shaw* states that a Black soldier was hanged at the Sun River and buried at a nearby slaughterhouse because he was not permitted to be interred in the Soldiers' National Cemetery. For more on Black soldiers in Montana, see Anthony W. Wood, *Black Montana: Settler Colonialism and the Erosion of the Racial Frontier, 1877–1930* (Lincoln: University of Nebraska Press, 2021).

The following indicated quotations come from: "Accident": Reyhner and Eder, *American Indian Education*, 134, 132. "Sites": Klopotek, "Preface," *Indian Subjects*, Kindle location 122. "Political": Child and Klopotek, "Introduction," *Indian Subjects*, 4. The photograph described comes from: "Teachers & Pupils— 1910," in Daisy, *An Indian School Diary* (1908, typescript print 1975), MHS. The author notes that this diary "of the final years and closure of the Fort Shaw,

Montana, Industrial Indian School, was given to her by her grandfather Henry J. Kinley. I found statements about the runaway capture payments in: Daisy, *Indian School Diary*; *History of Fort Shaw*, 10. The "Prank" story and quotation comes from *History of Fort Shaw*, 11.

On Mary Fields, I consulted: Dee Garceau-Hagen, "Finding Mary Fields: Race, Gender, and the Construction of Memory," in *Portraits of Women in the American West*, ed. Dee Garceau-Hagen (New York: Routledge, 2005), 122, 139, 143 ("wagon master" quote), 145; Annie Hanshew, "The Life and Legend of Mary Fields," in *Beyond Schoolmarms and Madams: Montana Women's Stories*, ed. Martha Kohl (Helena: Montana Historical Society Press, 2016), 78–81; Wood, *Black Montana*, 51–53.

For the history of women's basketball, I consulted: Peavy and Smith, *Full-Court*, 15–17. Mary-Beth Cooper, "Where Basketball Was Invented: The History of Basketball," Springfield College, springfield.edu.

For an example of a northern plains woman warrior, see: Edwin Thompson Denig, "Biography of Woman Chief," *Five Indian Tribes of the Upper Missouri: Sioux, Arickaras, Assiniboines, Crees and Crow* (Norman: University of Oklahoma Press, 1975), 195–200.

For the concepts of wildness and vitality, I took cues from the following texts. Ella Deloria, "Health Education for Indian Girls," *The Southern Workman* 53 (February 1924): 63–64. In a section at the end of her report where she charges modern Native girls with lacking morals, Deloria writes about community controls that were traditionally placed on girls' movement after the onset of puberty, including exploring far from the village alone and riding in the company of boys (67–68). Waggoner's views as interpreted here come from: Josephine Waggoner, manuscript notebook, courtesy of Lynne Allen; Josephine Waggoner, *Witness: A Hunkpapha Historian's Strong-Heart Song of the Lakotas*, ed. Emily Levine (Lincoln: University of Nebraska Press, 2013), xvii. I am grateful to Emily Levine, who shared her insights on Waggoner's views of nature and the plains. Emily Levine to Tiya Miles, May 4, 2022; quoted with permission. To interpret this material, I turned to and quoted Leanne Betasamosake Simpson, *As We Have Always Done: Indigenous Freedom through Radical Resistance* (Minneapolis: University of Minnesota Press, 2017), 151, 150, 154.

For the material on boarding schools and sports, I relied heavily on Beth Eby's original research in Eby, "Building Bodies, (Un)Making Empire: Gender, Sport, and Colonialism in the United States, 1880–1930," PhD diss., University of Illinois, 2019, 19, 80–82, 87–88, 93–95, 101. I also relied heavily on Deloria, "Health Education for Indian Girls," 63–68, to which Eby introduced me; Deloria notes that playing games could help distract boarding school girls from "the pangs of homesickness" (65). I borrowed from Philip J. Deloria, *Indians in Unexpected Places* (Lawrence: University of Kansas Press, 2004), 109–135. I also drew on John Bloom, *To Show What an Indian Can Do: Sports at Native American Boarding Schools* (Minneapolis: University of Minnesota Press, 2000), 22, 28, 103, 125. The argument that participation in athletics was a means of "escape" for girls at boarding school has also been made by Beth Eby; Eby, "Building Bodies," 7. Beth Eby has observed that the same bloomers that lent white women greater flexibility at the turn of the twentieth century were more confining than Native women's dress. Beth Eby, invited presentation in the course "Native American Women: History and Myth," taught by Tiya Miles with teaching fellow Sarah Sadlier, Harvard University, March 30, 2021. She has also noted that female student athletes in sex-segregated spaces were wearing gym suits by the 1890s and bloomers by 1900, but that they continued to wear skirts when playing in public (Eby, "Building Bodies," 36–37). Ella Deloria mentions the contrast between Native women's clothing of the past, which was "suitable" for exercise, and the "constricting garments" of early-twentieth-century mainstream women's culture ("Health Education," 63). For more on bloomers versus "home clothes," see Lomawaima, *Prairie Light*, 95–96.

On blackface: Peavy and Smith, *Full-Court*, 241, 401–402 footnote 10. At the Cherokee Female Seminary, a school founded and run by Cherokee people for Cherokee students, blackface was also adopted in student performances. The historian Devon Mihesuah discusses this practice in relation to the school's approach of distancing Cherokee identity from blackness. Devon A. Mihesuah, *Cultivating the Rosebuds: The Education of Women at the Cherokee Female Seminary, 1851–1909* (Urbana: University of Illinois Press, 1993), 83–84. Racial headline and description: *Anaconda Standard*, November 23, 1902; cartoon: *Butte (Mont.) Inter Mountain*, November 28, 1902; Peavy and Smith, *Full-Court*, 408 footnote 15, 120. Healy as quoted in Peavy and Smith, *Full-Court*, 156. Genevieve Healy did not play in this match. She performed during the entertainment as part of the mandolin club.

The Sacagawea statue at the fair, created by Bruno Zimm, a New York artist, did not survive. Michael Heffernan and Carol Medlicot, "A Feminine Atlas? Sacagawea, the Suffragettes and the Commemorative Landscape in the American West, 1904–1910)," *Gender, Place and Culture: A Journal of Feminist Geography* 9, no. 2 (2002): 109–131, 112, 115. For my discussion of the St. Louis fair, I consulted Nancy J. Parezo and Don D. Fowler, *Anthropology Goes to the Fair: The Louisiana Purchase Exposition* (Lincoln: University of Nebraska Press, 2007), 2 ("massive" quote), 3, 6, 10, 12, 143–144. I also relied on and quoted from Danika Medak-Saltzman, "Transnational Indigenous Exchange: Rethinking Global Interactions of Indigenous Peoples at the 1904 St. Louis Exposition," *American Quarterly* 62, no. 3 (2010): 591–615, 593, 608. I consulted Susan Brownell, "Introduction: Bodies before Boas, Sport before the Laughter Left," in *The 1904 Anthropology Days and Olympic Games: Sport, Race, and American Imperialism*. ed. Susan Brownell (Lincoln: University of Nebraska Press, 2008), 3–5. I quoted from Adams, *Education for Extinction*, 211–213. "Little ladies" is as quoted in Peavy and Smith, *Full-Court*, 233. James Sullivan was the director of Physical Culture, and W. J. McGee was the director of the Anthropology Department for the fair. The superintendent of the Model Indian School was Samuel McCowan; he was also the superintendent of Chilocco School. The basketball coach who convened the challenger team was Philip Stremmel.

The Memory book details come from: Peavy and Smith, *Full-Court*, 266; Linda Peavy and Ursula Smith, "World Champions: The 1904 Girls' Basketball Team from Fort Shaw Indian Girls Basketball School," *Montana: The Magazine of Western History* 51 (Winter 2001): 20–25, 22. The team oral history information derive from Peavy and Smith's interviews with family members (especially pp. 347–362).

For the Meriam report, see Lewis Meriam, Technical Director, *The Problem of Indian Administration*, Institute for Government Research Studies in Administration (Baltimore: Johns Hopkins University Press, 1928). In 2022, the first Native American secretary of the interior, Deb Haaland (Laguna Pueblo), issued a report on boarding school history as part of her department's Federal Indian Boarding School Initiative. Bryan Newland, Assistant Secretary Indian Affairs, "Federal Indian Boarding School Initiative Investigative Report," May 2022.

CONCLUSION: BLUE MOONS

For Huerta, I consulted: Stacy K. Sowards, ¡Sí Ella Puede!: The Rhetorical Legacy of Dolores Huerta and the United Farm Workers (Austin: University of Texas Press, 2019), 36. The "Strong" quote comes from Dolores Huerta Girl Scout Patch, Dolores Huerta Foundation, www.girlsoutshcc.org.; Kemp (Kathryn) Stockton (Calif.) Girl Scouts Collection, 1937–1956, Mss202, 1.6 Girl Scout Scrapbook, 1937–1956, Holt-Atherton Department of Special Collections, University Library, University of the Pacific. For Boggs, I consulted and quoted from: Grace Lee Boggs, *Living for Change: An Autobiography* (Minneapolis: University of Minnesota Press, 1998), 12, 13, 15, 25; Grace Lee Boggs, with Scott Kurashige, *The Next American Revolution: Sustainable Activism for the Twenty-First Century* (Berkeley: University of California Press, 2011), 115, 105, 18.

For the material on Butler, I read and quoted from the sources that follow. "'Honey, You Got a MacArthur': Blacks Who Have Received Genius Grants," *Journal of Blacks in Higher Education* no. 17 (Autumn 1997): 67–68. Randall Kenan, "An Interview with Octavia E. Butler," *Callaloo* 14, no. 2 (1991): 495–504, in *Conversations with Octavia Butler*, ed. Consuela Francis (Jackson: University Press of Mississippi, 2010), 27. Nivea Serrao, "Octavia Butler's Sci-Fi Classic 'Kindred' in the Works at FX, as NASA Honors Beloved Author with Mars Landing Site," March 9, 2021, syfy.com. Joan Fry, "Congratulations! You've Just Won $295,000: An Interview with Octavia Butler," in *Conversations with Octavia Butler*, 126. Quoted in Lynell George, *A Handful of Earth, a Handful of Sky: The World of Octavia E. Butler* (Los Angeles: Angel City Press, 2020), 155. Susan Palwick and Octavia Butler, "Imagining a Sustainable Way of Life: An Interview with Octavia Butler," *Interdisciplinary Studies in Literature and Environment* 6., no. 2 (Summer 1999): 149–158, 151. Julie Dash interview with Octavia E. Butler, Forty Acres and a Microchip Film Conference, 1995, https://vimeo.com/163190768.

From the Butler Papers, I read and referred to: "Silver Star" (also "Flash"), horse story and drawings/map, Octavia E. Butler Papers, OEB 2472, Box 129, Huntington Library, San Marino, CA (hereafter HL). Copyright © by Octavia E. Butler. Reprinted by permission of the Octavia E. Butler Estate. Commonplace Books, Small, 1993–1995, OEB 3129, Box 168, Octavia E. Butler Papers, HL. Copyright © by Octavia E. Butler. Reprinted by permission of the Octavia E. Butler Estate. Octavia E. Butler and a large tree, Frances D. Louis Collection Photographs, Octavia E. Butler Correspondence and Photographs, 54, Box 2, 80704, Octavia E. Butler Papers, HL. Octavia E. Butler to George W. Bush, circa 2001, Octavia E. Butler Papers, Correspondence, Box 208, 3821, HL. Copyright © by Octavia E. Butler. Reprinted by permission of the Octavia E. Butler Estate. I also read and quoted from her published fiction: Octavia E. Butler, "The Book of Martha," An Exclusive Short Story from Octavia Butler in Celebration of Her Birthday (New York: Seven Stories Press, 2018), www.sevenstories.com; Octavia E. Butler, *Parable of the Sower* (New York: Warner Books, 1993), 49.

After hearing a virtual lecture I gave at Carleton College in 2021, a student asked if I see any contemporary Harriet Tubmans. I said Tubman was an extraordinarily unusual (though fully human) historical figure and cited the author Clint Smith as noting that people like her came along "once in a blue moon." I borrow that phrase from Smith again in the epilogue. ("Driven by the Living Past," a panel discussion with Farah Jasmine Griffin, Tiya Miles, and Clint Smith, Brooklyn Book Festival, October 3, 2021.)

EPILOGUE: TREE TOPS

For my discussion of outdoor play and pandemic green space, I drew from the sources that follow. Gabriela Bento and Gisela Dias, "The Importance of Outdoor Play for Young Children's Healthy Development," *Porto Biomedical Journal* 2, no. 5 (2017): 157–60, 158, https://doi.org/10.1016/j.pbj.2017.03.003. Eva Änggård, "Children's Gendered and Non-Gendered Play in Natural Spaces," *Children, Youth and Environments* 21, no. 2 (2011): 5–33, 27. See also Margaret J. B. Currie, Petra Lackova, and Elizabeth Dinnie, "Greenspace Matters: Exploring Links Between Greenspace, Gender, and Well-Being with Conservation Volunteers," *Landscape Research* 41, no. 6 (2016): 641–651. Fritz Kleinschroth and Ingo Kowarik, "COVID-19 Crisis Demonstrates the Urgent Need for Urban Greenspaces," *Frontiers in Ecology and the Environment* 18, no. 6 (2020): 318–319, 319. J. D. Wortzel, D. J. Wiebe, G. E. DiDomenico, et al., "Association between Urban Greenspace and Mental Wellbeing during the COVID-19 Pandemic in a U.S. Cohort," *Frontiers in Sustainable Cities*, 3 (2021): 2, 1, 5. Ian Leahy and Yaryna Serkez, "Since When Have Trees Existed Only for Rich Americans?" *New York Times*, June 30, 2021. Lincoln R. Larson, Lauren E. Mullenbach, Matthew H. E. M. Browning, et al., "Greenspace and

Park Use Associated with Less Emotional Distress among College Students in the United States during the COVID-19 Pandemic," *Environmental Research* (2021): 112367, 7.

For discussions of the links between the encroachment of green space, climate change, and the spread of disease, see: Abrahm Lustgarten, "How Climate Change Is Contributing to Skyrocketing Rates of Infectious Disease," *ProPublica*, May 7, 2020. "Coronavirus and Climate Change," Center for Climate, Health, and the Global Environment, Harvard T. H. Chan School of Public Health, https://www.hsph.harvard.edu/c-change/subtopics/coronavirus-and-climate-change/.

FURTHER READING

CHAPTER 1: STAR GAZERS

Cahill, Loren S. "BlackGirl Geography: A (Re)Mapping Guide Towards Harriet Tubman and Beyond," *Girlhood Studies* 12, no. 3 (2019): 47–62.

Clinton, Catherine. *Harriet Tubman: The Road to Freedom* (2005). A compelling account of Tubman's individual story and a "sweeping, historical" vision of the underground railroad.

Dunbar, Erica Armstrong. *She Came to Slay: The Life and Times of Harriet Tubman* (2019). A lively, accessible, and illustrated tribute to Harriet Tubman.

Field, Corinne T., and LaKisha Michelle Simmons, eds. *The Global History of Black Girlhood* (2022).

Glave, Dianne D., and Mark Stoll, eds. *To Love the Wind and the Rain: African Americans and Environmental History* (2005). A vivid, invaluable collection of essays that sheds light on the relationship between African Americans and the environment in US history.

Jacobs, Harriet. *Incidents in the Life of a Slave Girl* (1861). An in-depth, first-person account of Jacobs's life as an enslaved woman and her quest to gain freedom for herself and her children.

Larson, Kate Clifford. *Bound for the Promised Land: Harriet Tubman: Portrait of an American Hero* (2004). A richly detailed biography of Harriet Tubman as a complete human being—"brilliant, shrewd, deeply religious, and passionate in her pursuit of freedom."

McKittrick, Katherine. *Demonic Grounds: Black Women and the Cartographies of Struggle* (2006). A critical interpretation of Black women's geographic thought and places, including Harriet Jacobs's attic, negotiated by Black women during and after the Atlantic slave trade.

McKittrick, Katherine. "Plantation Futures," *Small Axe* 17, no. 3 (42) (2013). McKittrick theorizes the enduring connections between the geopolitics of slave plantations and contemporary Black dispossession in urban contexts.

"Tubman 200," the Harriet Tubman Bicentennial Project by *Ms. Magazine*, https://msmagazine.com/tubman200/. An online initiative honoring the bicentennial of Harriet Tubman's birth, with essays on Tubman's manifold contributions to feminism and justice, conversations with Tubman's descendants, a reparations calculator, and original art and poetry.

CHAPTER 2: NATURE WRITERS

Cahill, Cathleen. *Recasting the Vote: How Women of Color Transformed the Suffrage Movement* (2021). A narrative-supplanting account of the battle for enfranchisement, highlighting the leadership of antiracist activists, including Gertrude Simmons Bonnin (Zitkála-Šá).

Cooper, Brittney C. *Beyond Respectability: The Intellectual Thought of Race Women* (2017). A multifaceted, cutting-edge history of Black feminist intellectual tradition and political action from the 1800s to the 1970s.

Fields, Mamie Garvin, and Karen Fields. *Lemon Swamp & Other Places: A Carolina Memoir* (1985). A first-person account of Mamie Garvin Fields's childhood in Charleston, South Carolina, and the wider social landscape of the segregationist South of her youth, coauthored with her sociologist granddaughter Karen.

Fiege, Mark. *The Republic of Nature: An Environmental History of the United States* (2013). A broad reconceptualization of US history in terms of climate, resources, and organic cycles.

Jones, Martha. *Vanguard: How Black Women Broke Barriers, Won the Vote, and Insisted on Equality for All* (2020). A rigorous and vibrant history of Black women's leadership in the suffrage movement and transformation of American political life.

Morrison, Toni. "The Site of Memory," in *Inventing the Truth*, edited by William Zinsser (1995). Morrison's canonical exploration of the temporal and natural movement of memory and the tools used in Black literature to insist on Black humanity in the face of systemic dehumanization.

Sentilles, Renée M. *American Tomboys, 1850–1915* (2018). An extensive cultural history of nineteenth-century girls who took pleasure in rowdiness and shaped US history with their gender-bending freedom.

CHAPTER 3: GAME CHANGERS

Child, Brenda J. *Boarding School Seasons: American Indian Families, 1900–1940* (2000). A nuanced and emotional history of Indian boarding schools in the early twentieth century, braided with the revealing letters between parents and children profoundly impacted by these institutions in both positive and negative ways.

Deloria, Philip J. *Indians in Unexpected Places* (2004). A collection of essays about the "unexpected" images of Native Americans that reveals settlers' stereotyped visions of Native experience as well as Native engagement with modernity.

Garccau-Hagen, Dee. *Portraits of Women in the American West* (1995). An anthology of biographical essays about women in the American frontier that offers valuable insights on gender in the nineteenth-century United States.

Lomawaima, K. Tsianina. *They Called It Prairie Light: The Story of Chilocco Indian School* (1995). A pathbreaking and widely assigned historical account offering cutting-edge analyses of boarding school dynamics and highlighting the voices of Chilocco Indian School students, who speak about their experience living and learning on the off-reservation boarding school from the 1920s to the 1930s.

INDEX

Page numbers in *italics* refer to illustrations.

"To the Pine Tree" (Schoolcraft), 64
trachoma, 91
transcendentalist literary movement, 36
tree canopy, poverty and, 127–28
trees, 120, *121*
tribal languages, prohibition of, 87
tuberculosis, 91
Tubman, Harriet, 13–22, *30*, 41, 81, 90,
    113, 123
  birth of, 17
  brain injury of, 28
  ecological consciousness of, 7–8
  enslaved people led to freedom by, 31
  escape of, 29–32
  Haviland compared to, 38–39
  L. M. Alcott and, 49
  name change of, 28
  self-expressive legacy of, 15
  significance of nature for, 27, 39–40
  significance of star shower to, 27
  value of nature for, 15–17, 125
  woodsman skills of, 29–32
Tubman, John, 28
Turner, Nat, 1831 rebellion of, 34
Twain, Mark, 8
25th Infantry Black regiment, 85

"Uncle Jeff" (Black man), 37
Underground Railroad, xiv, 13, 22, 31, 49
  Haviland's role in, 38–39
*Undrowned: Black Feminist Lessons from
  Marine Mammals* (Gumbs), 113
United Farm Workers Union, 116, *117*
urban development, 126
urban forestry, 127
urban garden movement, 115
urban greenspaces, 127
Ursuline order, 90
Ute people, 93

vanishing Indian trope, 60
Victorian era:
  gender ideology, in, 5, 8, 10, 41–43, 45,
    48, 49, 53, 56, 75, 98–99

  women's restrictions in, 41
Victorville, Calif., 119
Virginia, 57
"vitality," use of term, 96
Voice from the South, A (Cooper), 62, 70
voting rights, for women, *see* suffragists,
  suffragist movement
Voting Rights Act (1965), 62
Waggoner, Josephine, 96–97, 98
Walden; or, Life in the Woods (Thoreau),
  48
Walden Pond, 47, 48
Walking Trees (Jackson), *129*
Walton-Raji, Angela, 25
Washington, DC, suffrage parade in, 61
water:
  literary significance of, 68–69
  in Tubman's girlhood, 13
weeds, Tubman's self-association with, 14
Wells, Ida B., 61
"White Girls against Reds" (article headline), 104
whites, *see* Euro-Americans
"Who Gets Left Out of the 'Great Outdoors' Story?" (Finney), 1
Wilder, Laura Ingalls, 97
"wild freedom," as Native American tradition, 95–96
wildness:
  rhetoric of, 96–98
  use of term, 7
Winslow, William, 76–77, 89–90, 92
"winter bridge," xiii
Wirth, Lizzie, 93
Wirth, Nettie, 93, *101*, 111
*Woman's Life-Work, Labors and Experi-
  ences, A* (Haviland), 37
women:
  as abolitionists, 8
  abuse of, 82
  as athletes, 73
  masculinized image of, 90–91
  restrictions on, 6–7, 70, 100
  suppression of, 11

Norton Shorts

BRILLIANCE WITH BREVITY

W. W. Norton & Company has been independent since 1923, when William Warder Norton and Mary (Polly) D. Herter Norton first published lectures delivered at the People's Institute, the adult education division of New York City's Cooper Union. In the 1950s, Polly Norton transferred control of the company to its employees.

One hundred years after its founding, W. W. Norton & Company inaugurates a new century of visionary independent publishing with Norton Shorts. Written by leading-edge scholars, these eye-opening books deliver bold thinking and fresh perspectives in under two hundred pages.

Available Fall 2023

Wild Girls: How the Outdoors Shaped the Women Who Challenged a Nation by Tiya Miles

Against Technoableism: Rethinking Who Needs Improvement by Ashley Shew